We Are Disturbed

Letters From The Edge

G000059780

Nicola Joy and Karina Evans

Crombie Jardine
PUBLISHING LIMITED
Office 2, 3 Edgar Buildings
George Street
Bath
BA1 2FJ
www.crombiejardine.com

Published by Crombie Jardine Publishing Limited
First edition, 2006

ISBN 1-905102-86-0 (10-digit)

ISBN 978-1-905102-86-0 (13-digit)

Design by www.glensaville.com
Printed and bound in Great Britain by
Cox and Wyman Ltd, Reading, Berks

CONTENTS

ONCE UPON
A TIME

Once upon a time, several moons ago, two young, nubile, gorgeous, intelligent, socially aware, down to earth, friendly, sane and generally Goddess-like females realised that their lives were not going according to plan. So, they climbed off their spiritual toadstool and set out with their associates on a mission to rectify this. During this journey, things went wrong. The results are shocking. Pages upon pages of disturbed, ranting crap ...

A NOTE FROM THE AUTHOR

As well using our real names in the following letters, we felt the need to adopt some pseudonyms to cover our trail. These ordinary sounding names will ensure that no harassment orders are taken out against us. Our addresses have been blurred out to protect the innocent*. This is primarily to avoid irate company representatives, Andrew Lloyd Webber, mutant inbreds and Colin Farrell** turning up on our doorstep and shaking their angry fists/extremities at us in the manner of short-changed pensioners.

* By innocent we really mean guilty.
** Although we really wouldn't mind, Colin, if you bring some vodka, disinfectant, a chainsaw and a board game.

Section 1

In the beginning we complained a

lot

SHARKY SHORTBOTTOM
WILHELMINA LONGBOTTOM
BOTTOMS DOWN

02 March 2006

Vlavidar Vodka Company
Glasgow
Scotland
G2 5RG

Dear Mr Vlavidar

We recently happened upon an off licence, where we purchased, against our better judgement, a litre of Vlavidar vodka. We rushed home, cracked open the bottle, and proceeded to pour ourselves healthy measures. We thoroughly enjoyed these healthy measures and so decided to drink some more. We drank with gay abandon. Then some oddities occurred. Firstly, we became unsteady on our feet and crashed into some useful ornaments, thus rendering them useless. Then, to our horror, the room started to spin. We shouted 'STOP THE BUS', but to no avail. We then decided to go out for a walk to clear our scrambled minds. Unfortunately, by this point, there were two of everything. We walked through the wrong doorway, thus resulting in large and painful bruises on and about our persons. We then felt strange rumblings in our stomachs and projectile vomited all over each other, thus resulting in a fight and more large and painful bruises. We then passed out and awoke with an unusual craving for greasy foods. We have now gained 1lb in weight, thus rendering us fat.

We have since discovered that all of the above symptoms can be encompassed under the umbrella called drunkenness.

We are writing to you to suggest that you incorporate a warning upon your bottles stating that alcohol may make you drunk.

We look forward to hearing from you soon.

Yours with saggy bottoms and diseased livers,

Sharky Shortbottom (The Shark)

Wilhelmina Longbottom (The Willy)

WHYTE & MACKAY
GLASGOW

8ᵗʰ March 2006

Mr. ▮ ▮▮▮▮▮▮▮▮
▮▮ ▮▮▮▮ ▮▮▮▮▮
▮▮▮▮▮▮ ▮▮▮▮ ▮▮▮

Dear Mr. Shortbottom,

We were distressed to read of the dreadful experiences of yourself and Ms Longbottom with a bottle of Vladivar Vodka. By the time we finished reading your letter the tears were running down our cheeks. Some even wet themselves resulting in dry cleaning bills being sent to the company.

As a responsible drinks company we are signatories to The Portman Group's Code of Practice with regard to drink promotion. At the same time we have always considered the British public to be a responsible bunch unlike our American cousins. The Arses of Burns Rush USA require warnings from the Surgeon General about the dangers of alcohol consumption, but surely not descendants of William the Conqueror. Are you related to la Petite Derriers of Normandy by any chance?

It did cross our minds that it would be inappropriate to reward your efforts with more alcohol, especially in view of your liver condition. However perhaps your recent experiences have taught you a lesson and you can now be classed as responsible drinkers. So under separate cover we are arranging to send a complimentary bottle to you, please drink it in moderation and savour all the hard work that has gone into making this fine vodka.

We are not in a position to assist with weight loss and suggest you contact your local Weight Watchers who we understand may run a joint course with your local Alcoholics Anonymous Club at reduced rates for couples.

Please accept our thanks for writing to tell us of your exciting life we never realised drinking Vladivar could be such fun.

Yours sincerely,

Compliance Manager (soon to be replaced)

SHARKY SHORTBOTTOM
WILHELMINA LONGBOTTOM
BOTTOMS DOWN

12 March 2006

Vlavidar Vodka Company
Glasgow
Scotland
G2 5RG

Dear ▓▓▓▓▓▓ (soon to be replaced),

We were saddened to hear of the unfortunate mass temporary incontinence that occured in your office upon receipt and perusal of our letter. Although generally marketed at females, there are products on the market that can assist you in avoiding the wet pant scenario that you all recently found yourselves in. We apologise. We do hope that your incontinence is not the reason that you are 'soon to be replaced' This, we feel, is discrimination, and there are places you can go who will sue your employers on your behalf if this is the case.

We are in no way related to la Petite Derrieres of Normandy, although Wilhelmina is a quarter Dutch, and Sharky has a friend in Finland.

Unfortunately we have found ourselves in a very difficult situation with the litre bottle of Vlavidar vodka that you sent us. We no longer live at the same address, and due to the argument about the useless ornaments, and the bruises that subsequently appeared, we no longer drink together. For this reason, we are asking if you would kindly forward us an extra bottle of Vlavidar vodka, so that we can both enjoy our own vodka, responsibly, in the privacy and safety of our separate abodes.

Thank you again for your kind offerings, we look forward to hearing from you soon.

Yours,

THE 'SHARK'

THE 'WILLY'

PS. We encourage you to seek out a solicitor, don't forget-no win, no fee.

WHYTE & MACKAY
GLASGOW

27th March 2006

Dear Sharky and Wilhelmina,

I feel I know you well enough by now for first names and a break with formality.

Your concern for my well being is greatly appreciated. Purely in the interests of investigation I tried out your female solution over the weekend. Unfortunately they are very difficult to fit especially after a dose of Viagra which I take for accident prevention, it stops you from rolling out of bed after too many malts. Being accident prone yourself you should perhaps give it a try.

I am sorry to hear of your split. But you really must kiss and make up, where else will you find someone with the same warped sence of humour. Now personally I would be delighted to send you a whole case of Vladivar never mind a bottle. However Vlad the Bad a close relative of Atilla the Hun has withdrawn my authority to gratis issue. Which leads me to my other predicament.

After finding out that I had responded to your first letter and sent you a bottle it was decided that I was going senile. This is my last day as tomorrow I am being sent to the home for the bewildered with no access to a solicitor. My replacement has been appointed, young, heartless, no sence of humour, built like a tank and worse of all a Glaswegian Rangers supporter.

So fare well dear friends I hope your life goes on.

Now what all this piddle is really saying is, don't push your luck, quit while you are ahead, your fishing line is broke.

It has been fun corresponding with you.

Yours sincerely,

Compliance Manager

8 – 21 SALAMANDER PLACE LEITH EDINBURGH EH6 7JL

T ▨▨▨▨▨▨▨   F ▨▨▨▨▨▨▨   WHYTEANDMACKAY.COM

WHYTE AND MACKAY LIMITED REGISTERED OFFICE DALMORE HOUSE 310 ST VINCENT STREET GLASGOW G2 5RG
REGISTERED IN SCOTLAND NO. SC014456 VAT REGISTRATION NO. 596 6187 11

KARINA EVANS AND NICOLI JOY

4 November 2003

Mr R McDonald
McDonalds Restaurants Plc
11-59 High Road
East Finchley
London
N2 8AW

Dear Mr McDonald

After a recent afternoon in therapy, myself and my good friend Nicoli happened upon our local McDonalds, where we decided, against our better judgement*, to purchase a Cheeseburger™. Upon my first bite I discovered, with great horror, that my Cheeseburger™ did not house a gherkin. I tried, in vain, to stop my good friend Nicoli opening her Cheeseburger™, only to discover, with horror, that she had already done so. I only had to see the look of dismay upon her face to realise that her Cheeseburger™ also did not house a gherkin. After a moments stunned silence we discussed, at great length, the options open to us. These options I have listed below:

Should we:

A/ Throw the Cheeseburgers™ onto the floor in disgust and grind them to a pulp with our hiking boots and wellingtons.

B/ Throw our arms in the air in dismay, therefore making it apparent to all in company that our Cheeseburgers™ did not house gherkins.

C/ Bravely confront the cheeky McDonaldette, who was, apparently, `lovin' it`, who sold us the aforementioned naked Cheeseburgers™.

We decided upon option C. We did not take this decision lightly, so you can imagine our horror when upon confrontation with aforementioned cheeky McDonaldette about aforementioned Cheeseburgers™, she did not even attempt to hide her mirth. She laughed in our face, then snidely offered us a whole gherkin, which you can imagine, would be quite a mouthful. We declined her sarcastic offer and wheeled around on our hiking boot/wellington clad foot. My other mouth then uttered the immortal words 'I will <u>not</u> be back' before marching purposefully out of my own personal hell. Straight into a slippery puddle.

My therapist has since informed us that this visit has set us back a good year.

Yours with gay abandon and trauma,

UEvans

Karina Evans

NJoy

Nicoli Joy

* Our better judgement informed us that McDonalds Cheeseburgers™ only contain 10% cow, processed vegetables, chicken testicles and 10,000 calories.

As we heard nothing from McDonalds, we sent the original letter again along with the following letter. Yet still we heard nothing.

KARINA EVANS AND NICOLI JOY

8 December 2003

Mr R McDonald
McDonalds Restaurants
11-59 High Road
East Finchley
London
N2 8AW

Dear Mr R McDonald,

With reference to the enclosed letter. We are utterly disgusted with your appalling customer services. Nobody ignores us.

NOBODY.

Grr.

We look forward to hearing from you soon.

Yours with anger, frustration and uncontrollable rage.

Karina Evans

Nicoli Joy

PEOPLE'S PIES

JD Wetherspoon plc
PO Box 616
Watford
WD24 4QU

7 November 2003

Dear Mr Wetherspoon,

We recently happened upon a local Wetherspoon's establishment where we ordered, against our better judgement, two calorie laden double Baileys™. The barmaid in question did not realise that the frivolous purchase was an attempt to show the general public our drinking stamina, and proceeded to put the shots into comically large glasses. This made our vast shots of Baileys™ look like a piddly drip in the ocean, thus leaving us embarrassed and humiliated.

We are writing to you to ensure that this humiliating and degrading bar service does not occur again.

Cheers,

Nicola Joy

Karina Evans

J D WETHERSPOON plc PO BOX 616 WATFORD WD24 4QU
DX122490 WATFORD 4
TELEPHONE: ▮▮▮▮ FAX: ▮▮▮▮
www.jdwetherspoon.co.uk

cw.bp.ml71699/1806
14 November 2003

▮▮▮▮
▮▮▮▮
▮▮▮▮
▮▮▮▮
▮▮▮▮

Dear Ms Evans

Thank you for your letter of 7th November 2003 and for taking the time to write to us.

I am concerned to hear that you were not satisfied that your Baileys were served in our new glass tumblers at The John Logie Baird. Generally if the staff are made aware of your dissatisfaction, steps will be taken to rectify this by changing the glasses the drink is served in. I have passed your comments of disappointment regarding all the issues raised to the Area Manager concerned to investigate. I can assure you, your comments will be given serious consideration and the relevant action will be taken. The Area Manager will ensure the staff are reminded of good customer service at all times and whilst rare, that any future mistakes are rectified to the customers satisfaction.

Once again, I apologise that this incident occurred and I do appreciate you writing to bring this to our attention. I can assure you that this is not indicative of the service we aim to give our customers. We have taken your comments seriously and I do hope you will not be deterred from visiting us again soon

Yours sincerely

Julie Dare
CUSTOMER SERVICES

NICOLI JOY AND KARINAI EVANS

8 December 2003

Masterfoods UK
Melton Mowbray
Leicestershire
LE13 0BR

Dear Mr Mowbray,

We recently chomped our way through an extra large box of Celebrations because we are greedy and could not wait for Christmas. Merry Christmas by the way. Anyway, as we were a-chomping, horror overwhelmed us...because the milky way wrappers were crap. Yes, shite. Utter codswallop. Veins were pulsating wildly in our temples as we, three grown men, a midget with a wooden spoon and a gimp with a crowbar attempted to prise the wrapper from the sweet. But to no avail. Milky ways happen to be the midget's favourite sweet, so he became angry and chased and prodded us with his wooden spoon for a good half a mile, whilst roaring with sheer frustration. He will be forwarding his therapy bill. As will my mother.

Please find enclosed offending milky way with mohican-like wrapper. Why do you not twiddle your sweets like everyone else? Our lives are hard enough without having to cope with you and your crap wrappers.

We look forward to hearing from you soon.

Yours with sore fingers and a hatred of wooden spoons,

Nicoli Joy

Karinai Evans

17 December 2003

Our Ref: 1289197A

A Division of Mars U.K. Limited
Mill Street
Melton Mowbray
Leicestershire LE13 1BB

Dear Sirs

I am sorry to hear that you have not been satisfied with some Celebrations. Thank you for bringing this to our attention, we value feedback from our customers regarding product quality.

We take customer comments very seriously, and it is genuinely helpful to receive feedback on all aspects of our products from consumers. As a company, we are proud of the reputation we have achieved over the years for high quality and reliability. We have many quality systems in place, and every precaution is taken in the design, preparation, manufacture, packaging and distribution of all our products.

Please accept my apologies for any inconvenience which may have been caused. I enclose complimentary reimbursement to the value of £2.00 which will enable you to purchase some more Masterfoods products. Please accept this with my compliments. I do hope this has not affected your confidence in our products, and that you will continue to use Masterfoods products and remain one of our valued customers.

Yours sincerely

Mrs Justine Bayldon
Consumer Quality Advisor
Direct Line - 01664 416974

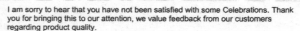

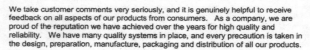

T _____ , F _____ - www.mars.com

Registered at the Companies Registration Office: London, England - Registered number 696458 - Registered Office: 3d Dundee Road, Slough SL1 4LG
MASTERFOODS is a trademark

**K EVANS
N JOY**

20 November 2003

Hastings Borough Council
Town Hall
Queens Road
Hastings
East Sussex
TN34 1QR

Dear Mr S Hump,

We are writing with regard to the excessive speed humpage in and around the Hastings area. Myself and my good friend Nicoli were a-strolling after a recent evening 'on the lash'. It was dark and the street lighting was a little dim, so we inadvertently found ourselves walking in the road. Imagine our shock, horror and utter confusion when a speed bump loomed and attacked us viciously around the ankle area, thus resulting in grazed knees, broken sunglasses and a dirty bandana. We laid spread-eagled, arms and legs akimbo, in stunned silence. We said 'What the f*@!?' before composing ourselves, getting up, walking onwards, and tripping over another. This time an ugly man let out a squeal of amusement, thus adding to our shame, humiliation and degradation.

It is therefore our suggestion that you put warnings on and around your speed humpage, thus ensuring that this does not happen to another innocent stroller.

We look forward to hearing from you soon,

Yours with unnecessary trauma,

Karina Evans

Nicoli Joy

Transport and Environment

Robert E Wilkins
MSc CEng MICE MInstWM MIHT
Director

Peter Gosnay
FIHIE IEng
Highway Manager
Hastings Area

Century House
100 Menzies Road
St Leonards on Sea
East Sussex
TN38 9BB

Telephone Hastings ▓▓▓▓ ▓▓▓▓

Fax ▓▓▓▓ ▓▓▓▓

East Sussex County Council

▓▓▓▓▓▓▓▓▓▓
▓▓▓▓▓▓▓▓▓▓
▓▓▓▓▓▓▓▓▓▓
▓▓▓▓▓▓▓▓▓▓
▓▓▓▓▓▓▓▓▓▓

date
15 December 2003
your ref

when responding please contact
Angela McEwan
Telephone ▓▓▓▓ ▓▓▓▓

our ref
C/M/C1/AM/JN

Dear Ms Evans

INCIDENT INVOLVING TRAFFIC CALMING MEASURES

Thank you for your letter dated 20 November 2003 regarding the above incident.

In order to be able to investigate this further, we will require the location where your accident occurred.

Should you wish to provide us with this information, we would be happy to look into the matter.

Thank you for your co-operation.

Yours sincerely

P J Gosnay

P J GOSNAY
HIGHWAY MANAGER

cc   A McEwan

T:\MS Word\Julie\PJG\Evanslet.doc

Hastings
BOROUGH COUNCIL

Hastings Borough Council
Highway Management Contractor
to East Sussex County Council

**K EVANS
N JOY**

30 December 2003

Hastings Borough Council
Town Hall
Queens Road
Hastings
East Sussex
TN34 1QR

Ref: C/M/C1/AM/JN

Dear Mr Angela McEwan,

With regard to the above incident. We were 'on the lash', and so cannot recall where this incident occurred. Please could you send a map pinpointing all your speed humpage, so we can refresh our memories.

We would also like to take this opportunity to reprimand you on your hideous choice of council builders/roadworkers. None of them are fit; they all have saggy, hairy buttocks peeping out of their low slung trousers. We are disappointed and frankly quite disturbed at the sight of these aesthetically challenged beings adorning our roads. We would appreciate it if you could amend this oversight immediately.

We have enough crap and stress in our lives without having to look at men who have obviously been lightly hit with the ugly stick.

Give us something pretty.

Yours,

K Evans

N Joy

PEOPLE'S PIES

20 November 2003

Consumer Quality Manager
Trebor Bassett Ltd.
Freepost Mid 20061
Birmingham
B30 2QZ

Dear Mr C Eclair.

We recently purchased several large packets of chocolate eclairs. Our eyes were not too big for our bellies and we proceeded to scoff the whole lot. Yes, you are reading correctly, THE WHOLE LOT. Except one lone eclair that presented itself to us in a manner not pleasing to the eye. The eclair in question was housed in a mutant wrapper which was twiddled at one end and not the other, thus leaving the eclair's naked, bald head clearly visible to all around. If the eclair in question had feelings, and we believe they do, it would be deeply disturbed by it's shoddy, exposing, humiliating attire. It is no better than dressing a slapper in fishnets.

We are therefore returning the traumatised eclair for counselling and redressing. We expect you to return our eclair dressed in an appropriate manner as soon as possible.

We look forward to being reunited with our eclair and to hearing from you soon.

Yours with sweet teeth and rumbling stomachs.

Nicoll Joy

Karina Evans

CADBURY LTD.

27 November 2003

PO BOX 12
BOURNVILLE
BIRMINGHAM B30 2LU
CONSUMER DIRECT LINE
SWITCHBOARD TELEPHONE
www.cadbury.co.uk
FAX No.

Our Ref:- 1027014A

Dear Ms Evans,

I am very concerned that you had cause to contact us about Cadbury's Chocolate Eclairs, and I would thank you for taking the time and trouble to bring this matter to our attention.

Trebor uses the latest high speed wrapping machines. Very occasionally, the flow of product into the wrapping machine can be slowed or stopped to allow for minor adjustments to be made.

Incorrectly wrapped product that has passed through the wrapping system will as a matter of course be removed. In this instance it is clear that at least one of the products escaped detection.

Please accept our apologies for the disappointment and inconvenience caused. I hope you will use the attached refund for £2.00 to purchase and enjoy further supplies of Trebor Bassett's confectionery. Thank you once again for taking the trouble to contact us.

Yours sincerely

p.p Susan Browning TM3
Consumer Relations Department

PEOPLE'S PIES

15 December 2003

Susan Browning
PO Box 12
Bournville
Birmingham
B30 2LU

Ref: 1027014A

Dear Ms Susan Browning,

With reference to the above. We were very disturbed, distraught, agonised and traumatised to discover that the letter we received from you did not contain our appropriately dressed eclair. We have a few questions for you:

Where is our eclair?

Have you kidnapped it?

Is it safe?

What is the ransom?

Is it still cold?

Is it clean, or covered in fluff?

Is it dressed in appropriate attire, or is it still in it's shoddy, humiliating, exposing mutant wrapper?

We cannot believe that we sent our eclair to you in blind trust, believing that it would be returned safely, yet you believe that a measly £2 voucher is adequate compensation for the loss of such a close friend.

PLEASE RETURN OUR ECLAIR and clear your conscience. Please find enclosed your blood money.

Yours with disgust and the constabulary in tow,

NICOLI JOY

KARINA EVANS

CADBURY LTD.

PO BOX 12
BOURNVILLE
BIRMINGHAM B30 2LU
CONSUMER DIRECT LINE
SWITCHBOARD TELEPHONE
www.cadbury.co.uk
FAX No.

12 January 2004

Our Ref:- 1027014B

Dear Ms Evans,

Thank you for your letter which has been passed to me for response.

I was equally concerned to learn of your recent traumatic experience with one of our Chocolate Eclairs. This must have been the cause of a great deal of distress to yourselves and please be assured we were forever grateful to you for letting us know your tale of woe.

However, as with any 'rogue' sweets that should not find their way into packs and escape our Quality Assurance department your Eclair has been dealt with and we were unable to return it to you as I am afraid to say he no longer exists!

Please be assured our Quality Team are more vigilant than ever since your complaint and we hope not to repeat a similar experience!

Thank you for contacting us, I have taken the liberty of sending you an additional voucher and trust you will use this to purchase some top of the range Chocolate Eclairs with our very best wishes.

Yours sincerely

Jane Potts
Consumer Relations Department

PEOPLE'S PIES

Sheridans
Customer Services
Guiness UDV UK
Park Royal Brewery
NW10 7RA

Dear Mr and Mrs Sheridan,

We recently purchased, against our better judgement, a standard sized bottle of Sheridans two toned alcoholic beverage. We excitedly opened the Sheridans and read the instructions. which we followed to a tee. Imagine our dismay, horror and utter disbelief when, upon pouring the two toned alcoholic beverage, as stated on the bottle, we realised that, disturbingly, it was not pouring as pictured. The white substance got carried away with itself and poured faster than the brown liquid thus leaving us with half a bottle of brown liquid and little white substance left. We were utterly flabbergasted. We resorted to putting a (clean) finger over the offending opening orifice in order to make the liquid pour evenly.

We have therefore come to the conclusion that your instructions are a pile of codswallop.

Yours with gay abandon,

Karina Evans

Nicoli Joy

Our Reference 6528/6931/12998

DIAGEO

GREAT BRITAIN

18 November 2003

Consumer Relations
PO Box 2
Oxon
OX9 3GN

Spirits & wines:
Tel

Guinness brands:
Tel

Kaliber
Tel

diageo.info@diageo.com
Fax

Dear Ms Evans

Thank you for your recent letter regarding Sheridan's.

Before progressing further, we need to determine whether or not it is necessary to analyse the product at our Brand Technical Centre and, if so, provide them with the required information.

Therefore, we would appreciate it if you would answer the following questions either by return with this letter or by telephoning us.

1) Do you still have the bottle in your possession?

2) If yes, how much is left in the bottle?

3) What is the size of the bottle?

4) What is the Best Before Date on the bottle?

5) What is the LOT number on the bottle?

6) When was the bottle purchased?

7) Have you consumed/purchased this Brand before?

8) Did you notice anything unusual about the liquid or packaging before opening it?

9) When was the product first opened?

10) Has it been opened since then?

If you are unable to provide this information within one week of receipt of this letter, please let us know.

Yours sincerely,

C White

Chris White
Consumer Relations

Our Reference 6528/6931/12998

18 November 2003

DIAGEO

GREAT BRITAIN

Consumer Relations
PO Box 2
Oxon
OX9 3GN

Spirits & wines:
Tel

Guinness brands:
Tel

Kaliber
Tel

diageo.info@diageo.com
Fax

Dear Ms Evans

Thank you for your recent letter regarding Sheridan's.

Before progressing further, we need to determine whether or not it is necessary to analyse the product at our Brand Technical Centre and, if so, provide them with the required information.

Therefore, we would appreciate it if you would answer the following questions either by return with this letter or by telephoning us.

1) Do you still have the bottle in your possession? *No! we smashed it against the wall in blind fury!*

2) If yes, how much is left in the bottle? *Just a large stain upon carpet*

3) What is the size of the bottle? *LARGE*

4) What is the Best Before Date on the bottle? *Hang on, let me reconstruct it.. 50/20/3781*

5) What is the LOT number on the bottle? *A.R.S.E. 100*

6) When was the bottle purchased? *6th EphiphiNiki*

7) Have you consumed/purchased this Brand before? *Every Morning Mixed with Warm Cider*

8) Did you notice anything unusual about the liquid or packaging before opening it? *Slight green tinge*

9) When was the product first opened? *In the shop upon purchase.*

10) Has it been opened since then? *Please reread Question 1.*

If you are unable to provide this information within one week of receipt of this letter, please let us know.

Yours sincerely,

C Unice

we look forward To hearing from you soon Mr White

Chris White
Consumer Relations

Mr White, are you incharge of the white section of Sheridans two toned liqueur?

DIAGEO

GREAT BRITAIN

Consumer Relations
PO Box 2
Oxon
OX9 3GN

Spirits & wines:
Tel

Guinness brands:
Tel

Kaliber
Tel

diageo.info@diageo.com
Fax

Our Reference 6528/6931/13095

25 November 2003

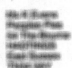

Dear Ms Evans

Thank you for your recent letter contacting us regarding Sheridan's.

In order for us to investigate a product concern, we need to carry out an analysis at our relevant Brand Technical Centre. Unfortunately, as you have indicated that you no longer have the bottle, this is not possible and, therefore, we cannot progress any further. However, we do log all incidents of this type for reference against similar occurrences.

We would ask that, in future, you retain any product and contents in order that we can take the appropriate steps to deal with your concern in a more satisfactory manner.

Yours sincerely,

Chris White
Consumer Relations

Diageo Great Britain is a trading name
of Diageo Great Britain Limited

Registered office: 8 Henrietta Place
London W1G 0NB
Registered in England and Wales
No. 507652

PEOPLE'S PIES

09 November 2003

Mr Beans
Highfield Drive
Churchfields Industrial Estate
St Leonards
East Sussex
TN38 9UB

Dear Mr Bean

We recently happened upon a Mr Beans coffee shop where, against our better judgement, we ordered 2 smoothies and two cream cakes. Upon choosing these items from the vast array of goodies available, we ventured towards the counter. Imagine our shock, horror and utter dismay when the woman serving at the counter started bellowing at us in a rather gravelly tone. We had done nothing to deserve this dressing down, which scared us as we are of a naturally nervous disposition. We can think of no reason as to why she shouted 'NEXT PLEASE!' at us in an aggressive manner. We approached the counter with trepidation, scared as to what the deviant may do next, when she charged us a staggering £2.40 each for the smoothies, and an utterly unbelievable £1.75 each for the cakes. The cakes, although pleasing to the eye, were not pleasing to the tastebuds. We were very disappointed with the service, the price, the taste of your products, and the aggression of your staff. Should we happen upon a Mr. Beans in the future, we will listen to our better judgement and walk on by.

Yours with gay abandon and trauma,

Nicoli Joy

Karina Evans

OVENMILL LTD.

T/A The ten sixty six Bakery. Mr.Bean Coffee Houses and The 1066 Sandwich Company

Head Office : Highfield Drive, Churchfield Ind Est, St.Leonards on sea, East Sussex, TN38 9UB

Telephone █████████ Fax █████████ E-mail: █████████

Wednesday 12 November 2003

█████████
█████████
█████████
█████████
█████████
█████████

Dear Mr Joy & Miss Evans

Having received your letter with reference to complaints re: our prices and the attitude of the staff member you were served by, I will obviously find the latter complaint difficult to address to the staff member in question, as you have mentioned no date or time that you frequented the site.

I have spoken to my site Manager, re: your complaint, and he will be speaking to each member of staff about their customer service skills; as 'next please' in an aggressive manner is certainly not what we expect from any of our staff, and could be a disciplinary matter.

The prices for the products you purchased are justifiable prices, as are all the prices we charge in our sites, so am unable to appologise for this, but am disappointed that you feel the cakes were not 'pleasing to your taste buds,' as we always receive very good reports about our products.

Thank you for taking the time to write to us, as any comment or complaint helps us to improve or think about our customer relations and products.

Yours sincerely

Miss T D Robertson
Managing Director

Company Registration No 2370330

PEOPLE'S PIES

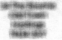

03 November 2003

Golden Virginia
PO Box 83
Nottingham
NG7 5PR

Dear Mr G Virginia,

We recently happened upon a tobacconist and, against our better judgement, entered and, after much discussion, proceeded to purchase two large pouches of Golden Virginia tobacco.

Upon opening our Golden Virginia tobacco, we discovered several foreign objects lurking in the pouch. We studied these at great length and discovered that they were, in fact, large twigs. We said 'What the f*@?!', and proceeded to roll ourselves a cigarette. Upon rolling, one of the aforementioned offending twigs pierced our cigarette paper, leaving a small yet noticeable hole, thus rendering our roll up useless.

We were also, yet again, horrified, disgusted and utterly dismayed to discover straggly bits of tobacco had attached itself on and around our persons and in our bags. It reminded us of a Christmas tree shedding its pine needles as we are still finding them now. We are not festive people. We also found an offending straggly bit of tobacco upon our toilet seat. As we are both blonde, we believed it to be the pube of an intruder and promptly called the constabulary. Upon arriving and verifying that the offending straggle was, in fact, tobacco, the constabulary proceeded to degrade and humiliate us in front of our neighbours.

We strongly believe that you should incorporate these events into warnings upon your products so that other consumers do not frivolously waste police time and good money on twiggy, straggly tobacco. Please find some suggestions for these warnings on the attached sheet.

We look forward to hearing from you soon

Yours with gay abandon and trauma,

Karina Evans

Nicola Joy

<u>WARNING</u>

WARNING: Stray, straggly bits of tobacco may bear an uncanny resemblance to pubes. Please be aware that they are not pubes and are, in fact, stray straggly bits of tobacco.

WARNING: Stray twigs may be a-lurking inside this packet. They may damage your hand rolled cigarette, leaving a small yet noticeable hole, thus rendering it useless and unsmokeable.

WARNING: If you do not incorporate a filter into your hand rolled cigarette, straggly bits of tobacco may choke you.

Imperial Tobacco

IMPERIAL TOBACCO LIMITED
CONSUMER SERVICES
PO Box 61, Nottingham NG7 5QQ
Tel:
Fax:

17 November 2003

Dear Ms Evans,

<u>Golden Virginia</u>

We were sorry to learn that a recent purchase of our brand was found to be below our usual high standard.

We would like to assure you that every effort is made to ensure that all our products leave the factory in perfect condition. However, as you did not return the faulty product and packet, our Quality Controllers are unable to fully investigate the circumstances leading to your complaint.

We are pleased that you smoke our brand and trust that future purchases will not give rise to further complaint.

Please accept the enclosed with our compliments in recompense for any inconvenience caused.

Yours sincerely,

Miss M. O'Rourke

Enclosures:

25g Golden Virginia
1 First Class Stamp

Our Ref: 171971

 INVESTORS IN PEOPLE

www.imperial-tobacco.com
An IMPERIAL TOBACCO GROUP company
Registered in England No: 1860181 Registered Office: PO Box 244, Upton Road, Bristol BS99 7UJ

Certificate No.
FM25995
Cigarette Manufacture

NICOLA JOY
KARINA EVANS

11 February 2006

Red Bull Company Ltd.
14 Soho Square
London
W12 3QG

Dear Mr Wings,

We recently purchased, against our better judgement, vast quantities of Red Bull.
Upon returning home to our fifth floor apartment, we consumed aforementioned
vast quantities of Red Bull, to our detriment. After consuming three litres apiece, we
took to our windowsills, jumped, and began flapping frantically. But alas, for the
promised wings did not sprout. Imagine our shock, horror and utter fright when we
noticed that the flower bed was approaching rapidly. We flapped frantically for a
good two and a half seconds, but to no avail. The mess was phenomenal; all our
pansies had been squashed and our herbaceous border was no more. Shame on
you for putting adverts upon the television promising us wings. We are writing to
suggest that you incorporate these events into a warning on your packaging, and
make it clear on your advertisements that Red Bull does not give you wings. Stop
lying to us.

Thank you for your time, we look forward to hearing from you soon,

Yours with wingless rage, squashed pansies and broken bones,

NICOLA JOY

KARINA EVANS

Red Bull

Red Bull Company Limited
14 Soho Square · London W1D 3QG
Tel: ███████ · Fax: ███████
www.redbull.com

███████████████████
███████████
█████████████
█████████
██████
█████████

19 February 2006

Dear Nicola & Joy,

Red Bull – Product Complaint

Thank you for your recent letter and for your feedback on Red Bull.

With regard to your concerns about not growing wings - it is true that Red Bull does give you 'wiiings' (as opposed to wings) but not in an obvious conventional manner but by vitalising your **body and mind**, as illustrated in our humorous self-ironic cartoons.

I dare say that in the history of evolution there has never been a case of a human being naturally blessed with real wings in the sense that you mean and Red Bull would not attempt to fool the general population at large into thinking that it was possible to drink our product and change their genetic make up to grow extra parts of the body!

I assure you that the style of the advertisements and message that they give have been passed by the Advertising Standards Authority and are deemed suitable for broadcasting to the viewing public. Furthermore, all of our advertising is scrutinised by lawyers before it is broadcast therefore I am sure they would have made sure that it complied with all necessary legislation on the subject.

I am sorry that you feel the message conveyed in our commercials misled you and your husband in any way into believing that Red Bull would persuade your body to sprout bird-like feathery appendages.

Please accept out sincerest apologies for any confusion you have may have suffered.

Yours sincerely

Nichola Spencer
Red Bull Company Limited

Registered Office: Torrington House · 47 Holywell Hill · St Albans · Hertfordshire AL1 1HD
Registered in England Number: 02790349

NICOLI JOY
KARINA EVANS

10 June 2005

Public Inquiries Business Center
NASA Headquarters
Suite 1M32
Washington, DC
20546-0001

Dear Mr Nasa,

The atmosphere has polluted our faces and made us spotty and blotchy. You have helped to pollute the atmosphere with your fuel guzzling space rockets. Therefore, it is your God given duty to rectify this.

We have heard on the grapevine that you have a spacious zero gravity chamber. This could be just what we need to restore our previously unblemished flesh blankets to their former glory. If you could kindly send us an invitation, we would happily float around your chamber in peace and tranquillity for five days and four nights. The results will be outstanding.

In return, we are willing to embark upon an important space mission for you, with our friend the gimp. We have enclosed a diagram of us dressed as astronauts. We are sure that by now you have reached the conclusion that this is a mutually beneficial exchange. It is a win-win situation.

Yours with oxygen deprived skin and wrinkly bottoms,

NICOLI JOY

KARINA EVANS

National Aeronautics and
Space Administration
Headquarters
Washington, DC 20546-0001

July 14, 2005

Public Affairs

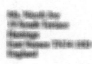

Dear Ms. Joy:

Thank you for your inquiry to the NASA.

The Web site, http://ec.msfc.nasa.gov/hq/library/unSol-Prop.html contains information on
how to submit a proposal to NASA. Basic information on theory submittal can be obtained at
http://imagine.gsfc.nasa.gov/docs/ask_astro/answers/960908.html.

We appreciate your interest in the Nation's space program.

Sincerely,

Public Communications Management Office
National Aeronautics and Space Administration

NICOLI JOY
KARINA EVANS

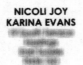

7 March 2006

Public Enquiries Business Center
NASA Headquarters
Suite 1M32
Washington DC
20546-0001

Dear Sir/Madam,

We wrote to you earlier this year, please find copies of the correspondence enclosed. We have perused the web pages that you suggested we look at regarding our proposal. It has taken us just over four months to trawl through to information contained on this web page, and we are still none the wiser. We put it to you, in writing, that you are attempting to disorientate us, in the hope that in our disorientated state we will forget to submit our proposal. But no, not us, no way. We will not be fobbed off, we will find a way. Will you please re-read our original proposal and submit it for us? Please let us know if this is a viable option.

Yours with square eyes,

NICOLI JOY

KARINA EVANS

PS. Please could you send us some complimentary oxygen packs to see us through the winter? We are suffering terribly.

Karina Evans and Nicola Joy

Humdinger Ltd
Gothenburg Way
Sutton Fields Industrial Estate
Kingston Upon Hull
HU7 0YG

08/07/05

Dear Humdingers,

Our neighbour Captain Fun dropped in for tea, stone out dates and a photo shoot for the local rag. Captain Fun's smile disappeared along with his tooth when he bit into one of your dates complete with stone. The warning on the packet is pathetically small and unfortunately Captain Fun is optically challenged. Maybe you should call your dates… Stone-in? Stone-out dates? Or how about Russian roulette dates?

Stones aren't fun and Captain Fun is no longer able to gnarl his teeth at small children.

Please find enclosed offending stone and packaging.

Karina Evans

Nicola Joy

PS When are you going to stop covering your dates in crappy vegetable oil? It's bad for one's health.

Food with Attitude

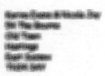

14 July 2005

Dear Karina & Nicola

<u>Customer Reference C314–05</u>

Thank you for your letter, dated 08 July 2005, regarding our Stone-out Dates (*BBE: March 2006 & Production Code: 5157H32 10:41*). We are sorry that you have had reason to complain about one of our products, and would like to assure you that we take all complaints very seriously.

The stones are normally removed during the preparation of the raw material. However, the method of removal of the stones from dates cannot be completely guaranteed, hence the warning on our packs, which is headed as a caution and the font is a different colour.

The vegetable oil used in this product is only used as a production aid, for ease of packing. Without this ingredient, the dates remain in clumps and are very difficult to work and pass through our machines. The amount of oil used in this product is kept to the bare minimum to enable us to process the raw material effectively, and is less than 1% of the total weight of raw material.

Again we are sorry that you have had reason to complain about one of our products, but we hope that you will remain a valued customer. Please accept the enclosed cheque as means of refund.

Yours sincerely

Emma Parkinson
Customer Care

Humdinger Ltd
Cothenburg Way
Sutton Fields Ind. Estate
Kingston Upon Hull
East Yorkshire, HU7 0YG

Tel:
Fax:

www.humdinger-foods.co.uk

vat: 772623226 company: 4241596

NICOLI JOY
KARINA EVANS

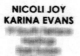

21 June 2005

Rexel
Acco UK
Gatehouse Road
Aylesbury
Buckinghamshire
HP19 8DT

Dear Mr Rex,

You have made us vexed. And slightly distressed. Once upon a time, about two days ago, we, three grown men, a midget with a wooden spoon, and a gimp with a crowbar, were compiling important papers for the Prime Minister. As we did not want the Prime Minister's important papers covered in coffee and bodily fluids again, after much discussion we had a brainwave. We should insert aforementioned paperwork into plastic sheaths. Your plastic sheaths. But shock horror. For they were not actually plastic sheaths, they had no orifices at either end, thus rendering them useless plastic bubbles. The gimp stared expectantly whilst we tried to insert a piece of paper into its sheath. The midget, blinded with fury, ran headlong into a door, rendering himself unconscious. Lucky for us, or he'd have given us a good beating with that spoon of his. Although that can sometimes feel quite nice.

Anyway, we digress. We have enclosed shoddy sheaths for you to insert orifices into and return to us.

Yours with disappointingly intact bottoms,

NICOLI JOY

KARINA EVANS

PS. Would you like to come round and spank us with a big old wooden spoon?

ACCO UK LIMITED
Gatehouse Road, Aylesbury,
Bucks. HP19 8DT, England

Telephone:
Fax:
E-mail:
www.acco.co.uk

Acco UK Ltd
Gatehouse Road
Aylesbury
Bucks
HP19 8DT

20th July 2005

Dear Nicoli & Karina

Sorry for the lateness of reply to your letter, this has been due to trouble matching pockets. The pockets that you sent us are of an older style and the new style is different in appearance. Unfortunately we are unable to obtain any of the old style and thus have enclosed a packet of the new pockets. I hope this resolves all your queries and we are sorry for distress this has caused you and your associates.

Yours Faithfully

Bryn Harper

Acco Customer Services Technology Channel

Registered Office:
Gatehouse Road,
Aylesbury,
Bucks. HP19 8DT,
England

Registered in England
No. 197754

NICOLI JOY
KARINA EVANS

4 August 2005

Acco UK Ltd
Gatehouse Road
Aylesbury
Bucks
HP19 8DT

Dear Bryn,

Budget pockets? After returning top quality but faulty sheaths, you compensate us with budget pockets? Unbelievable. We would never, ever use budget sheaths to protect the Prime Minister's important papers.

As we would not lower ourselves to use these we sent our associate, the gimp, out to purchase another box of top quality anti-glare sheaths. Which were surprisingly shiny. Upon completion of important paperwork, Captain Fun danced the Lambada in celebration. The gimp, furious that he was not doing the Conga, stamped his leather clad foot in protest. Straight on top of one of your slippery, shiny, shoddy sheaths. This resulted in a useless right leg and a squashed testis, which put him out of action for a whole week. Our midget has now regained consciousness after the last incident involving your product, and is now blinking against the bright sunshine.

Please fine enclosed offensive unwanted budget pockets and slippery sheaths.

Yours with glowing behinds,

NICOLI JOY

KARINA EVANS

PS. Do you have any shades?

KARINA EVANS & NICOLA JOY

Interbrew UK Ltd
Luton
LU1 3LS

31/08/05

G'day mate,

Your truly disgusting Castlemaine XXXX has ruined our night in. We write this as we sit upon a doorstep in Hastings, trying to stomach your amber mierda.

After polishing off a fine bottle of Pinot Grigio, we rummaged through the small yet handy alcohol fridge for remnants of nights gone by. Unfortunately, the male specimens of the house like beer, and not nice beer at that. At the back of the fridge, glowing like radioactive toxic waste, we came across a solitary can of Castlemaine XXXX. Upon consumption of the first mouthful we realised just what a mistake we had made. We coughed and we spluttered, thrashed around like goldfish out of water whilst turning a deeper shade of red by the minute. Truly disgusting, please remedy your formula immediately.

Yours with disturbed taste buds,

Karina Evans

Nicola Joy

InBev UK Limited

Porter Tun House
500 Capability Green
Luton, Bedfordshire
LU1 3LS
Tel
Fax
www.inbev.com

Our Ref: 000054162A

05 September 2005

Dear Karina and Joy

Thank you for contacting our Consumer Helpline regarding Castlemaine XXXX.

We are concerned this has happened to you and would like to conduct a full investigation. To enable our investigation to commence, please return the offending can in the pre-paid jiffy bag provided.

Once we have received the offending can an investigation will be carried out and we will write to you with the results.

If you are unable to return the product, please respond to this letter, by calling our **Consumer Helpline** within 10 working days from receipt of this letter on ████████████. Our office opening hours are Monday to Thursday 9am to 5pm and Friday 9am to 3.45pm.

On behalf of InBev UK Ltd, I would like to apologise for any inconvenience caused.

Yours sincerely

Helen Kenyon
Consumer Services Advisor
Enclosure

Registered in England and Wales, number 3982132.
Registered office: Porter Tun House, Capability Green, Luton, Beds. LU1 3LS U.K.

KARINA EVANS & NICOLA JOY

7 March 2006

Helen Kenyon
InBev UK Ltd
Porter Tun House
500 Cabability Green
Luton

Ref: 000054162A

Dear Ms Kenyon,

In response to your letter dated 05/09/05 and huge envelope. We cannot send you the offending can, as it in itself was not offensive.

We are actually feeling rather guilty about the previous letter we sent as there was nothing wrong with your product per se, it just did not suit our taste buds.

We would suggest you concoct additional formulae in order to cater for all taste buds. We would be willing to be employed as tasters for a large fee.

We apologise for any offence and inconvenience caused.

Yours truly,

KARINA EVANS

NICOLI JOY

KARINA EVANS
NICOLA JOY

12 September 2005

Consumer Service Department
Weetabix Limited
Burton Latimer
Kettering
Northants
NN15 5JR

Dear Sir/Madam,

Upon recent perusal of a box of your Alpen No Added Sugar we discovered that your salt controller may be slightly confused. Which in turn left *us* slightly confused. On the side of the box, it states that 100g of Alpen No Added Sugar contains 0.17g of sodium, yet conversely in the highlighted box it states that 40g of Alpen No Added Sugar contains 0.17g of sodium. Surely this cannot be the case, as it would be impossible for both measurements to contain equal amounts of sodium. Unless, of course, you are suggesting we sift through the extra salty bits and save them for later. If this is not the case then we therefore believe one of the statements to be false. Why do you feel the need to add such crap to your product anyway? Surely a few dates would suffice.

In order to remedy this confusion, we adjusted our ages, weights, builds and lifestyles accordingly on several occasions, which served only to make us even more confused.

One other thing that slightly confused us; Alpen contains cow's milk. Does this come from one blessed giant-uddered cow? If not we suggest you move your apostrophe.

Yours truly,

KARINA EVANS

NICOLA JOY

Reference: 304-73-0/ajl/V1.00

September 20, 2005

WEETABIX LIMITED
WEETABIX MILLS
BURTON LATIMER
KETTERING
NORTHANTS NN15 5JR

T:
T:
F:
e-mail:
web: www.weetabix.co.uk

Dear Ms Joy

Many thanks for your letter. Please allow me to explain.

The problem is one of coincidence. The conversion factor of sodium to salt is 2.5. In other words, you multiply the sodium figure by that number to obtain the salt figure.

It so happens the *sodium* content per 100g is 0.17g and the *salt* content per 40g work out to identical amounts, allowing for the omission of fractions of grammes.

I hope I have been able to answer your question and thank you again for giving us the opportunity to do so. It is always nice to hear from our friends.

Whilst we realise you did not write with monetary reimbursement in mind, we do hope you will accept the enclosed with our compliments.

Yours sincerely

Dan Herrin
Consumer Services Manager -

THE QUEEN'S AWARDS FOR ENTERPRISE 2004   Registered in England No: 267687 Registered Office: Burton Latimer, Northants   INVESTOR IN PEOPLE

The Weetabix product range

Alpen Apple & Blackberry with Yogurt Bar
Alpen Banana & Coconut with Milk Chocolate Bar
Alpen Fruit & Nut Bar
Alpen Fruit & Nut with Milk Chocolate Bar
Alpen Papaya, Pineapple & Chocolate Bar
Alpen Raspberry & Yogurt Bar
Alpen Strawberry with Yogurt Bar

Alpen Original
Alpen No Added Sugar
Alpen No Added Sugar with Apricots, Dates & Pistachios - *NEW!*

Ready brek Chocolate
Ready brek Original   - now also available in packs of 8 x 30g sachets

Seriously Oaty Spiced Apple & Sultana
Seriously Oaty Apple & Raspberry
Seriously Oaty Golden Honey
Seriously Oaty Thick & Tasty

Weetabix
Weetabix Organic

Weetabix Crunchy Bran

Weetabix Weetaflakes - *NEW!*   *A high fibre, low fat, wholegrain wheat & rice flake*

Weetabix Minis Banana Crisp
Weetabix Minis Chocolate Crisp
Weetabix Minis Fruit & Nut Crisp
Weetabix Minis Honey & Nut Crisp

Weetos

Weetos Cereal Bar
Weetos Honey Bar

20/09/05

KARINA EVANS
NICOLA JOY

8 October 2005

Dan Herrin
Weetabix Limited
Weetabix Mills
Burton Latimer
Kettering
Northants
NN15 5JR

Dear Dan,

In response to your letter, dated 20 September 2005, and pathetic offering of a £1 hush money voucher. We do not feel that this is adequate to compensate for the time we spent feeling very confused. Also, a £1 voucher does not even cover the cost of a new box of Alpen, therapy, or a salt sifter. It is not 1941, you know.

We are returning this voucher to you. Please find enclosed your measly offering; we do not want it. £3.75 would be much better.

Secondly, we still have not received a reasonable explanation for our cow/udder/apostrophe query. Does the 'cow's milk' come from one blessed giant-uddered cow, or not? If not, as stated before, you must correct this before the rampaging apostrophe police get you. Watch out, we hear that they are in another one of their rages.

Thank you for your time, we look forward to receiving our new voucher soon.

Yours truly,

KARINA EVANS

NICOLA JOY

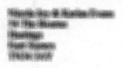

18/10/05

Bush Customer Services
Alba PLC
12 Thames Road
Barking
Essex
IG11 OHZ

Dear Sir/Madam,

Please find enclosed one shoddy DVD player manufactured by your company. The enclosed machine is refusing to power up; the fuse and the plug have been changed but to no avail. The DVD player was a brand new wedding present to ourselves in February 2004, and even though it has run past the standard one-year guarantee we expected more life from it than a measly nineteen months. We are very disturbed by this and so are our associates. Our good friends, the midget and the gimp, wanted to watch their favourite Trapdoor DVD the other evening and got irate when they couldn't. A fight then broke out between the pair, resulting in the gimp's facemask being ripped clean from his face, revealing his true identity. Very shocking indeed.

We look forward to receiving a very plausible explanation as soon as possible as to how and why this atrocity occurred, thank you for your time.

Yours truly,

Nicola Joy

Karina Evans

PS. The gimp would have tried to fix the DVD player himself; the idea of a nasty yet pleasant electrical shock excited him tremendously. He changed his mind at the last minute feeling it wasn't his time yet. We agree; he has so much left to do with his life.

Alba Radio Limited
Group Operations Division
12 Thames Road
Barking
Essex IG11 0HZ
England

t
f
www.albaplc.com

Please quote Our Ref: CS/28642

10 November 2005

Dear Ms Joy and Ms Evans

RE: BUSH DVD PLAYER. MODEL NO. DVD2023

We have received your DVD player and letter in our office on 9 November 2005.

We are sorry to read about the problem you have experienced with your DVD player.

Unfortunately, we do not have a repair service here however as a gesture of goodwill we can offer a replacement DVD player at the concessionary cost of £27.03 inclusive of VAT. This will be the same or an equivalent model.

To accept this offer please send a cheque in the sum of £27.03 made payable to Alba Radio Ltd to our Consumer Support Department at the above address.

On receipt of this payment, we will process your order.

Yours sincerely

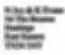

CONSUMER SUPPORT DEPARTMENT
HELPLINE NUMBER:

Registered Office
Harvard House 14-16 Thames Road
Barking Essex IG11 0HX England
Registered in England No 1639253

Directors

Secretary

Nicola Joy and Karina Evans

17/11/05

The Managing Director
Alba Radio Ltd
Group Operations Division
12 Thames Road
Barking
Essex IG11 OHZ

Ref: CS/28642

Dear Sir/Madam,

We recently returned a faulty DVD player to the consumer support department and after an age they finally replied with an appalling offer. The letter they sent, dated 10 November 2005, offered no explanation at all as to what was wrong with our DVD player, neither did it inform us of its current location. It just launched into a sales pitch trying to sell us another DVD player. We feel that this attitude is highly unacceptable and we would like an explanation of what went wrong with our DVD player. After you have finished examining it, we are assuming that you need to do this to improve future product and to find the explanation we require, we expect it to be safely returned to us with all its bits intact. While it is in your care please look after it, it has been away from us for a while now and may be feeling rather lonely. He has been a good friend to us; the thought of him rusting away in a reject warehouse distresses us greatly. His loss is even more pronounced after the gimp's speedy retirement to Brazil after last month's shenanigans.

Thank you for your time, we look forward to receiving an explanation and being reunited with our DVD player soon.

Yours truly,

Nicola Joy

Karina Evans

Alba Radio Limited
Group Operations Division
12 Thames Road
Barking
Essex IG11 0HZ
England

t
f
www.albaplc.com

Please quote Our Ref: CS/28642/2

1st December 2005

Dear Ms Joy and Ms Evans

RE: BUSH DVD PLAYER. MODEL NO. DVD2023

Thank you for your further letter that we received in our office on 23rd November 2005.

Your comments have been noted and as we advised in our previous letter to you, we do not have a repair service here therefore we will be unable to return the unit back to you in working condition.

We hope that the above information help in your enquiry and are returning the DVD Player with this letter. We regret that we are unable to help you further.

Yours sincerely

CONSUMER SUPPORT DEPARTMENT
HELPLINE NUMBER:
ENC

Registered Office
Harvard House 14-16 Thames Road
Barking Essex IG11 0HX England
Registered in England No 1639253

Directors

Secretary

Nicola Joy & Karina Evans

Consumer Support Department
Alba Radio Limited
12 Thames Road
Barking
Essex
1G11 OHZ

Our Ref:CS/28642/2

08/12/05

Dear Sir/Madam

With reference to your letter dated 1st December 2005. No, the above information does not help us with our enquiries, nor does it solve the fact that we still do not have a fully functioning DVD player. We do not want your pathetic excuses; we want a new DVD player and we want it now. We have asked Santa for lots of DVDs this year for Christmas and now we will not be able to watch them. How can you sleep at night? You should be ashamed of yourselves.

You obviously do not value your customers at all. You did not even take our machine apart to see what was wrong with it. Is that because you are lazy and do not care about the quality of your products? Or was it because you do not have the strength in your tiny arms to dismantle it, or lack the intellect to locate a screwdriver?

We would like a full report and investigation as to why we have been treated so unfairly and what caused our machine to fail after a measly nineteen months. We would also like a full refund of the postage it cost to send you our DVD player and a free replacement. We also ask that you forward a copy of this letter to the directors of your company.

Thank you for your time, we look forward to having our requests met soon.

Yours truly

Nicola Joy

Karina Evans

Nicola Joy & Karina Evans

26 January 06

Consumer Support Department
Alba Radio Limited
Group Operations Division
12 Thames Road
Barking
Essex
1G11 OHZ

Ref: CS/28642

Dear Rude People,

We sincerely hope that this will be the final letter that we have to send to you, because quite frankly we are bored with going over the same old ground.

We sent you a letter dated 08/12/05 and have been waiting in anticipation for our new DVD player and postage costs to be returned ever since. We have set up camp and have been waiting like morons by our letterbox for forty-nine days solid with only minimal food and water. We have only allowed ourselves a short break to write this letter.

Feel free to react with some courtesy and reply to this letter.

Yours,

Nicola Joy

Karina Evans

Please quote Our Ref: CS/28642/3

Alba Radio Limited
Group Operations Division
12 Thames Road
Barking
Essex IG11 0HZ
England

t
f
www.albaplc.com

3rd February 2006

Dear Ms Joy and Ms Evans

RE: BUSH DVD PLAYER, MODEL NO: DVD2023

Thank you for the further letter that we received in this office on 31st January 2006.

Your further comments have been noted and as explained in our previous letter to you dated 1st December 2005, we do not have a repair service here therefore we will be unable to repair your unit.

As your unit is over the 12 months warranty and there was no extended warranty taken out on the unit, you will need to contact a repair agent for a chargeable repair. However the repair cost may exceed the cost of the replacement unit (£27.03) that we offered you.

We hope that the above information helps in your enquiry and regret that you were unable to accept our gesture of goodwill offer.

Yours sincerely

CONSUMER SUPPORT DEPARTMENT
HELPLINE NUMBER:

Registered Office
Harvard House 14-16 Thames Road
Barking Essex IG11 0HX England
Registered in England No 1639253

Directors

Secretary

APLCGODL-1

Nicola Joy & Karina Evans

15 February 2006

Alba Spares Department
21 Thames Road
Barking
Essex 1G11 OHN

Dear people at Alba/Bush consumer support department,

We *would* like to say thank you for your letter dated 3rd February 2006 but that would be a blatant lie; we are not grateful at all, just thoroughly pissed off. Don't ever, ever, ever write to us again ever. Do you understand? All we wanted was a new bloody DVD player. For God's sake.

Yours with distain,

Nicola Joy

Karina Evans

Nicola Joy & Karina Evans

15 February 2006

Alba Radio Limited
Harvard House
14-16 Thames Road
Barking
Essex
1G11 OHN

Dear J E Harris MBE (Chairman)

Do you have any idea what your staff get up too? They have traumatised our associates, refused to inspect our faulty machine, refused to replace it and ignored us when we asked that our postage cost be refunded. We have enclosed copies of correspondance between ourselves and your consumer support department.

Nicola Joy

Karina Evans

DELIVERY NOTE

Alba PLC, Harvard House,14-16 Thames Road Barking, Essex, England, IG11 OHX   Page 1 Of 1
Tel: ▓▓▓▓ Fax: ▓▓▓▓

Load Number: ▓▓▓	POD Number: ▓▓▓ ▓▓▓▓

Collection Date: 2/03/2006
Carrier Code: UP   United Parcel Services

Collection Address W/hse: 1	Delivery Address
CORTONWOOD DISTRIBUTION CENTRE CORTONWOOD BUSINESS PARK CORTONWOOD DRIVE BRAMPTON, NR. ROTHERHAM SOUTH YORKSHIRE	▓▓▓▓▓ ▓▓▓▓▓ ▓▓▓▓▓ ▓▓▓▓▓ ▓▓▓▓▓

Load	D/Note	Customer Order No.	CAT No.	Item Code	Qty	Ctns	Plts
	▓▓▓▓▓▓▓			DVD2041SIL	1	1	0
DVD PLAYER							
				Page Total:-	1	1	0

Drivers Signature_____	**Customer Details** Cust Ref: STANDARD Del Date/Time: 3/03/2006 :
Drivers Name_____	Name_____
Trailer No._____	Signature_____
Vehicle Reg_____	Seal Nos_____ Please confirm above seal(s) was intact upon arrival initial & state Y/N._____

Subject to our standard terms & conditions.

Thank you Alba Radio Limited.

**NICOLA JOY
KARINA EVANS**

Twinings Head Office
South Way
Andover
SP10 5AQ

12 August 2005

Dear **SIR**,

Your passion for quality and dedication is tragically misguided. Although you're famous for selecting and blending a wide range of teas to suit all manner of moods and occasions, your bottles have made us bloody angry. The increase in price has infuriated us further. Gone are the cylindrical cardboard iced tea containers, which we are certain must be more environmentally friendly than your over priced, over tightened plastic vessels (please find enclosed). How can you justify the price increase with your utterly ludicrous new packaging? Who do you think you are? The Government? Put yourself in our position; feel the humiliation encountered when we had to enlist the help of a 4'9", gruff voiced, pseudo-woman to undo the ridiculously stiff screw top.

Yours Truly,

NICOLA JOY

KARINA EVANS

R.Twining & Co. Ltd
South Way, Andover,
Hampshire,
SP10 5AQ,
United Kingdom.
www.twinings.com

Tel:
Fax:

Ref:CIG/57/238

14 September 2005

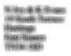

Dear Madam

We were most concerned to learn that your recent purchase of our Green Tea with Lemon Iced Tea was unsatisfactory.

We would advise that we always welcome customers' comments as they form an integral part of our ongoing programme to improve the overall quality of our products and your comments have been passed to the relevant personnel for consideration in the future development of this product range.

We thank you for bringing this matter to our attention and apologise for the inconvenience and disappointment caused. We are arranging to forward, with our compliments, some replacement product which we hope you will enjoy and which will restore your confidence in the quality of our products.

Yours faithfully

PP Toni Cohn.

Colin Gordon
Quality Assurance Manager

Registered In England No. 525071 Registered Office: Weston Centre, 3B Grosvenor Street, London W1K 4QY.

How generous they were; a box of twelve iced teas turned up on our doorstep a few days later. Unfortunately the pseudo woman was not around to help us open them.

**NICOLA JOY
KARINA EVANS**

27 June 2005

Complaints Department
South Eastern Trains
PO Box 125
Tonbridge
TN9 2ZA

Dear Sir/Madam,

It was a hot, sunny day. Last Thursday the 23rd of June to be precise. We had a mission; our mission was to get to London intact, on time, with consistently beautiful hair. But this was not to be; for from the outset your services were against us. The Gods of locomotives were definitely not shining down that day.

First of all, the 09.33 train from Hastings to London Charing Cross turned up 15 minutes late, throwing us into disarray. We had an important meeting. Very very very important. Half an hour into our journey, whilst we were sharing a really expensive Jaffa cake, a strange voice filled the air. We can only assume that this was the God of locomotives talking to us through the tannoy system. He told us that the train was late because your tracks had electrocuted an animal. We still do not know whether or not this was a deliberate act. We then disembarked to get on a train that was actually going to Charing Cross. As we stood there on the platform, we started to preen our hair using our reflections in the train window. Unfortunately, the train selfishly pulled away, thus resulting in Nicola's hair preened on one side and not the other, rendering her ugly.

And that's not all, for the horrors continued. We returned on the 18.15 train from London Charing Cross, which had a fault with the air conditioning system, to find ourselves sweating profusely in the manner of two thousand midgets in a mini.

We are disturbed. It is all your fault.

Yours sincerely,

NICOLA JOY

KARINA EVANS

 **south**eastern

South Eastern Trains
Customer Services
Admail 3920
London
SE1 1ZZ

Ref: 717544/SET - 1
08 July 2005

Dear Ms Joy and Ms Evans

Thank you very much for your letter received on 7 June 2005. I am very sorry to hear about the disruption to your journey when travelling from Hastings to London Charing Cross on 23 June 2005. We aim to run a reliable and convenient service but occasionally situations arise which are outside our control such bad weather, vandalism, security alerts or as on this occasion trespassing incidents.

The service you travelled on was affected by a animal running on the line. Whilst I understand your frustration, because the problem was beyond the control of the rail industry, we are not obliged to provide you with compensation on this occasion. I appreciate that this may seem unfair, but I can assure you that we do work hard to respond quickly when any kind of disruption to service occurs. However due to the problem with the air conditioning on your return journey I am able to consider a gesture of goodwill for your discomfort. To do this I require your journey tickets. Please send them to me at the following address quoting reference number 717544/SET-1:

Private and Confidential: Rebecca Bond
South Eastern Trains
Customer Relations
ADMAIL 3920
London
SE1 1ZZ

Thank you again for contacting South Eastern Trains and I hope future journeys are more successful.

Yours sincerely

Rebecca Bond
Customer Relations Advisor
South Eastern Trains Limited

Registered Office:
Friars Bridge Court, 41-45 Blackfriars Road,
London SE1 8PG
www.setrains.co.uk

Registered in England and Wales number 3666306

NICOLA JOY
KARINA EVANS

Rebecca Bond
Customer relations
Ad mail 3920
London
SE1 1ZZ

Ref 717544/set-1

Dear Rebecca

With reference to your letter dated 8/07/05. Please find enclosed proof of purchase of tickets to the value of £40.40. Thank you. Just when we were starting to trust in your services again, I was penalised for getting a train (the 7.48 to London Charing x) that arrived in London 10 minutes before 10 am. I was charged a whole extra £16.30. Being a student I cannot afford to be stung like this. I would have missed a lecture that started at 10am if I got a later train. This is disgusting, despicable, disturbing and wrong, wrong, wroooooooooOoong. Yes. Your. Company. Is. WROOoOng.

NICOLA JOY

KARINA EVANS

 **southeastern**

South Eastern Trains
Customer Services
Admail 3920
London
SE1 1ZZ
Tel:
Fax:
www.setrains.co.uk

Ref: 730546/SET
28 July 2005

Dear Ms Evans

Thank you for your letter of 08 July 2005. I am very sorry to hear about the disruption to your journey when travelling from Hastings to London Charing Cross on 23 June 2005. We aim to run a reliable and convenient service but occasionally situations arise which are outside our control such bad weather, fire, vandalism or security alerts.

The service you travelled on was affected by a dog being on the line ahead of your train. Whilst I understand your frustration, because the problem was beyond the control of the rail industry, we are not obliged to provide you with compensation on this occasion. I appreciate that this may seem unfair, but I can assure you that we do work hard to respond quickly when any kind of disruption to service occurs.

But due to the circumstances and the inconvenience caused I am happy to enclose £10.00 in Rail Travel Vouchers as a goodwill gesture. I do hope that you will be able to use these for another journey with South Eastern Trains, however they may be used towards a journey with any National Rail operator (including season ticket renewals) in the next 12 months.

In relation to your complaint about being charged more for travelling into London before 10.00. It is not that we increase the fare for peak time journeys, but that the standard fare is reduced where passengers are able to travel off peak or are willing to book in advance and restrict themselves to one specific service. This helps considerably with train planning, and with overcrowding, which is a problem despite the increase in the number of services.

Discounting rail fares for passengers who are able and willing to travel at less popular times helps to ensure that journeys are comfortable and that commuters are able to board the trains they need to reach their workplace at the correct time.

South Eastern Trains Limited

Registered Office:
Friars Bridge Court, 41-45 Blackfriars Road,
London SE1 8PG
www.setrains.co.uk

Registered in England and Wales number 3666306

I accept that this will be a disappointment. It would be nice to be able to reduce all rail fares, but we have to ensure that we are able to invest in new trains and services, and this does mean that fares must reflect the cost of running the service.

Thank you for telling us about your experience. It is only from feedback such as this that we are able to take action. It also helps us to identify trends or issues that we can then address.

Yours sincerely

John Dowse
Customer Relations Advisor

NICOLA JOY
KARINA EVANS

04 August 2005

John Dowse
Customer relations
South Eastern Trains
Ad Mail 3920
London
SE1 1ZZ

Ref: 730546/SET

A £10 travel voucher !!?? Take back your measly offer. You disgust us. We want our fairs and the dog back.

Nicola Joy

Karina Evans

 **southeastern**

South Eastern Trains
Customer Services
Admail 3920
London
SE1 1ZZ
Tel:
Fax:
www.setrains.co.uk

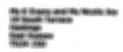

Ref: 751019/SET
12 August 2005

Dear Ms Evans/Ms Joy

Thank you for your letter dated 04 August 2005 in response to our previous letter regarding the delay to your train on the 23 June 2005. I can see that you are still unhappy that we have been unable to compensate you for the delay.

Your case has been reviewed by a Team Manager who has agreed with the response to you complaint. If you are still unhappy with our response you can escalate your case to the Rail Passengers Committee who can then review your case again for you. I have enclosed their address and contact telephone number for you below.

Rail Passengers Committee
Freepost WA1521
Warrington
WA4 6GP

Tel: 08453 022 022

Thank you for telling us about your experience. It is only from feedback such as this that we are able to take action. It also helps us to identify trends or issues that we can then address.

Yours sincerely

R Bond

Rebecca Bond
Customer Relations Advisor

South Eastern Trains Limited

Registered Office:
Friars Bridge Court, 41-45 Blackfriars Road,
London SE1 8PG
www.setrains.co.uk

Registered in England and Wales number 3666306

NICOLA JOY
KARINA EVANS

17 August 2005

Ref: 751019/SET

South Eastern Trains
Customer Services
Admail 3920
London
SE1 1ZZ

Dear Ms Bond. Rebecca Bond

In response to your letter dated 12/08/05, we were slightly...actually, we are not going to be polite; we were bloody furious. Stark raving mad. We appreciate that most of your money is spent on tannoy systems to announce delays to your services, the sick torture of small furry animals, and on dirty white handkerchiefs placed on the headrests in first class. Despite this, we feel that the compensation you sent us then cruelly stole away was inadequate and quite frankly insulting, considering the trauma we endured at your evil calloused hands. Do you know what it's like to feel ugly for the day?

Perhaps you could consider sending us a hundred pounds.

Yours faithfully,

NICOLA JOY

KARINA EVANS

PS. Can you please send us a copy of the last letter you sent to us as the fish ate ours? We need a copy for our records, and most probably court.

NICOLA JOY
KARINA EVANS

Rail Passengers Committee
Freepost WA1521
Warrington
WA4 6GP

17 August 2005

Ref: 751019/SET

Dear VIPs of the Rail Passengers Committee,

With reference to the above reference. We are appalled and need your assistance.
We know you can help us, as you are the Gods of the rail travel industry. We have
been humiliated, pilfered from, mocked shamelessly, and the dog's still dead.

We look forward to receiving our fares back in full.

Thank you for your time.

Yours faithfully,

NICOLA JOY

KARINA EVANS

Putting Passengers First...

RAIL PASSENGERS COUNCIL

5th Floor, Rail House, Store Street,
Manchester M1 2RP
Tel:
Fax:

Email:
Web:
www.railpassengers.org.uk

Your ref: 22ⁿᵈ August 2005
Our ref: 38877

Dear Ms Joy,

Complaint to the RPC Network

Thank you for your correspondence, which we received on the 22 Aug 2005.

The Rail Passengers Council and Committees are the statutory watchdog protecting and promoting passengers' interests. I see that you have been in touch with South Eastern Trains already and that you have contacted us because you are not satisfied with their reply. We describe this as an "appeal" complaint.

I would be grateful if you can summarise your complaint for me and explain what outstanding issues you have with South Eastern Trains. With this information, I will be able to review your complaint and if necessary make representation on your behalf.

Thank you for contacting the RPC network.

Yours sincerely,

Kyle Yeldon
Passenger Contact Advisor

Telephone:
Email:

INVESTOR IN PEOPLE

NICOLA JOY
KARINA EVANS

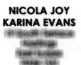

31 August 2005

Rail Passengers Council
Store Street
Manchester
M1 2RP

Ref 38877

Dear Kyle,

In reply to your letter dated 22 August 2005, the complaint and outstanding issues are as follows.

- We were late to our very important meeting; we nearly got sacked

- The air conditioning was broken; we overheated like 10,000 gimps in a sweaty dungeon

- The dog was electrocuted on the line. We were told about this in a disturbing way, which ruined the expensive jaffa cakes we were eating.

- We were only given a ten pound voucher between us as compensation, which they cruelly stole back (very tight we're sure you'll agree, it wouldn't even transport us over yonder hill)

- And last, but not least, we felt ugly for the day

We hope that you find this summary satisfactory and return our fares forthwith.

We look forward to receiving our fares soon.

Yours faithfully,

NICOLA JOY

KARINA EVANS

Putting Passengers First...

RAIL PASSENGERS COUNCIL
PASSENGER LINK CENTRE

9th Floor, Rail House,
Stone Street,
Manchester M1 2RP
Tel:

Email:

Web:
www.railpassengers.org.uk

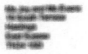

Ms Joy and Ms Evans
1st South Terrace
Hastings
East Sussex
TN34 4AB

Your ref: 13th September 2005
Our ref: 38877

Dear Ms Joy and Ms Evans,

Complaint to the RPC Network

Thank you for your letter of the 31st August 2005. I have contacted South Eastern Trains and I have been provided a full history of your case, which I have reviewed.

I understand that your journey on the 23rd June 2005 was delayed, as an animal was on the track. I appreciate the frustration the delayed caused however, SET are not liable for any further compensation. Under the National Conditions of Carriage, which forms the basis of the contract that you enter into when you purchase a ticket, it stipulates that train companies are not liable for any compensation for delays caused outside of their control.

In cases like yours, we rely upon gestures of good will, as there is not entitlement to any compensation. I understand that South Eastern Trains (SET) have provided a £10 rail voucher as a gesture in recognition of the delay and discomfort you encountered when using their service. I feel that the amount that has been offered is fair. Unfortunately, the RPC does not have the power to compel Train Operators to issue any larger gestures.

Chairman: Stewart Francis
National Director: Anthony Smith
Part of the RPC network - championing the interests of rail passengers

I am aware that this is not the outcome you sought, and I am sorry that the RPC cannot be of any further assistance to you. I hope that I have been able to clarify how and why we have reached this conclusion.

Yours sincerely,

Kyle Yeldon
Passenger Contact Advisor

Telephone:
Email:

NICOLA JOY
KARINA EVANS

17 September 2005

Rail Passengers' Council
9th Floor Rail House
Store Street
Manchester
M1 2RP

Ref: 38877

Dear Mr Yeldon,

Regarding your letter dated 13/09/05, we feel that the matter we brought to your attention has still not been addressed. South Eastern trains are still holding our compensatory rail travel voucher to ransom, and we would not be in the least bit surprised to find a threatening letter made from cut out pieces of newspaper text on our doorstep tomorrow morning. You may think that the sun shines out of their backsides, but we know differently. So, where is our ten pound voucher?

When you contact South Eastern trains regarding the return of our voucher, please make it clear to them that we are not attached at the hip, and after our last horrific train journey together, have absolutely no desire to ever travel together again. Ever. Therefore, two five pound vouchers would be more appropriate.

We will be forwarding this letter to Her Majesty.

Yours faithfully,

NICOLA JOY

KARINA EVANS

Putting Passengers First...

RAIL PASSENGERS COUNCIL
PASSENGER LINK CENTRE

9th Floor, Rail House,
Store Street,
Manchester M1 2RP
Tel:

Email:
Web:
www.railpassengers.org.uk

Your ref: 20th September 2005
Our ref: 38877

Dear Ms Joy & Ms Evans

Complaint to the RPC Network

Thank you for your letter dated the 17th September 2005.

From the case history I have received from South Eastern Trains, the voucher was returned to them in a letter from yourselves on the 4th August 2005. Nevertheless, I have spoken to South Eastern Trains, Customer Relations Department today, and they will be resending rail vouchers to the value of £10.00 to you.

If you have any further questions, or comments, please do not hesitate to contact me on

Yours sincerely,

Kyle Yeldon
Passenger Contact Advisor
Telephone:
Email:

INVESTOR IN PEOPLE

Chairman: Stewart Francis
National Director: Anthony Smith
Part of the RPC network · championing the interests of rail passengers

 **southeastern**

South Eastern Trains
Customer Services
Admail 3920
London
SE1 1ZZ
Tel: ███ ███ ███
Fax: ███ ███ ███
www.setrains.co.uk

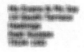

Ref: 762396/SET - 1
24 September 2005

Dear Ms Evans & Ms Joy

Thank you for your further contact. I have read through your previous correspondence and I am concerned to note that we have yet to reach a conclusion on this matter.

Please accept £ 10.00 in Rail Travel Vouchers as a goodwill gesture and I hope that you will be able to use these for another journey with South Eastern Trains, however they may be used towards a journey with any National Rail operator (including season ticket renewals) in the next 12 months.

Thank you again for contacting South Eastern Trains.

Yours sincerely

Sarah Booy
Customer Relations Advisor

South Eastern Trains Limited

Registered Office:
Friars Bridge Court, 41-45 Blackfriars Road,
London SE1 8PG
www.setrains.co.uk

Registered in England and Wales number 3666306

Rail Travel Voucher ≷

199
41008

1167

Issued by South Eastern Trains

Valid for 12 **months from** 24/09/2005

Notes

Ref 762396 **Value** £5.00 Five pounds

RECEIVING OFFICE

Ticket No. ....

Not valid if altered, defaced or
mutilated. Not transferable. Issued
subject to the National Conditions
of Carriage.

Please complete details overleaf

Bottomline Technologies / VCHO1
www.communisis-ep.com 9508

5556665

199 41008 5556665

Rail Travel Voucher ≷

199
41008

Issued by South Eastern Trains

Valid for 12 **months from** 24/09/2005

Notes

Ref 762396 **Value** £5.00 Five pounds

RECEIVING OFFICE

Ticket No. ....

Not valid if altered, defaced or
mutilated. Not transferable. Issued
subject to the National Conditions
of Carriage.

Please complete details overleaf

Bottomline Technologies / VCHO1
www.communisis-ep.com 9508

5556665

199 41008 5556665

**NICOLA JOY
KARINA EVANS**

17 September 2005

Her Majesty The Queen
Buckingham Palace
London

Dear Queen Elizabeth,

Do you have any idea what we, the general public, have to endure on a daily basis? We are sure that you do not, and so have enclosed some correspondence between ourselves, South Eastern Trains and the Rail Passengers Committee.

We are sure that you will agree that the service is in a diabolical state, something which needs immediate attention from yourself and Mr Blair. We think you should sack them all, and put us in charge instead. We will of course require a knighthood for this important role. We have knocked up out new titles below for your perusal.

Yours with awe,

SIR NICOLA JOY THE GREAT

SIR KARINA EVANS THE GREAT

Karina Evans & Nicola Joy

Consumer Services Department   04/11/05
Walkers Snack Foods Ltd
Po Box 23
Leicester
LE4 8ZU

Dear Sir/Madam

We were very shocked when we recently purchased a packet of Walkers max,
chargrilled steak flavoured, deep ridge potato crisps*. Upon the packet there was a
lone picture of one gigantic crisp, it was almost as big as one of our outstretched
palms. As we hadn't eaten for a while and were feeling ravenous, we thought that
these abnormally large crisps would satisfy us. We proceeded to buy several packets.
I cannot even begin to describe the disappointment that overwhelmed us when we
opened the packets only to discover the crisps were only a fraction of the size of the
aforementioned gigantic crisp. Upon closer scrutiny of the packet we discovered a
puny piece of text dwarfed by the giant crisp stating 'not actual size'. We think you
should enlarge this text so it is in proportion to the crisp, ensuring that this misleading
packaging does not fool other innocent consumers. You should be ashamed of
yourselves; we wish to know what you are going to do to correct this immediately.

Karina Evans

Nicola Joy

* Is it really necessary to have such long titles?

E/WK/05/12/1114/BP/270

15 November 2005

Customer Services

Freephone UK:
Freephone EIRE:
Direct Line:
Fax:

Dear Miss Joy

Thank you very much for your recent letter regarding our packaging.

We have forwarded your comments on to our Marketing Department for their consideration when a packaging review comes around and we would like to take this opportunity to thank you for taking the time and trouble to write to us.

Once again, thank you for taking the time and trouble to bring this matter to our attention.

Yours sincerely

Bhakesh Patel
<u>CONSUMER CARE ADVISOR</u>

Walkers Snack Foods Ltd

Feature Road, Thurmaston, Leicester LE4 8BS

Registered Office, 1600 Arlington Business Park, Theale, Reading RG7 4SA
Registered in England : No 2333054

Walkers Snack Foods Ltd may use the information you have supplied to contact you from time to time about its products and promotions which may be of interest to you. If you would prefer not to be contacted, please telephone our freephone number 0800 274 777 or alternatively e-mail us at Thurmaston.consumer@Walkers.co.uk advising that you wish to be deleted from our database and stating your name, address and reference number.

NICOLA JOY
KARINA EVANS

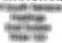

08 November 2005

Consumer Services Dept
Walker Snack Foods Ltd
PO Box 23
Leicester
LE4 8ZU

Dear Mr Square,

Upon opening a packet of your 'Square' brand potato snacks we discovered, with horror, that the description of these crisps was a blatant lie. Although 74% of the potato snacks were similar in shape and appearance to the aforementioned square, the other 26% were all, for want of a better term, rhombi. The sides were generally of equal length, but an unfortunate lack of right angles were noted by our mathematician. We also came across a 'Square' that looked uncannily like a flag blowing in the breeze. This is not strictly a rhombi, and so should not be treated as such, but we have enclosed it for your perusal. We would very much appreciate an explanation for this irregularity, as it has made us question everything we hold dear.

We look forward to hearing from you soon,

Yours sincerely,

NICOLA JOY

KARINA EVANS

C/WK/05/12/3129/PC/55

24 November 2005

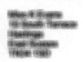

Customer Services

Freephone UK:
Freephone EIRE:
Direct Line:
Fax:

Dear Miss Evans

Thank you for your recent letter about Squares. I am sorry that you were disappointed with your purchase.

Every packet carries guidelines of what to do if you have an unsatisfactory product. By analysing any faulty product, we can find out exactly what went wrong and then correct the problem. Unfortunately, as we have received the packet but no contents, we are unable to fully investigate your complaint for you.

I am sorry that you were unable to enjoy your Squares. Thank you, once again, for contacting us and on this occasion, I enclose a voucher, with my compliments.

Yours sincerely

Pamela Crump (Mrs)
<u>CONSUMER CARE ADVISOR</u>

Enc. voucher £2.00

Walkers Snack Foods Ltd

Feature Road, Thurmaston, Leicester LE4 8BS

Registered Office: 1600 Arlington Business Park, Theale, Reading RG7 4SA
Registered in England : No 2333074

Walkers Snack Foods Ltd may use the information you have supplied to contact you from time to time about its products and promotions which may be of interest to you. If you would prefer not to be contacted, please ring our freephone number 0800 274 777 or alternatively e-mail us at Thurmaston.consumer@Walkers.co.uk advising that you wish to be deleted from our database and stating your name, address and reference number.

NICOLA JOY
KARINA EVANS

12 December 2005

Customer Services
Walkers Snack Food Ltd
PO BOX 22
Leicester
LE4 8ZU

Ref: C/WK/05/12/3129/PC/55

Dear Sir/Madam

With reference to your letter dated 24 November 2005. Thank you for your voucher,
but we are sending it back. Please find it enclosed. We feel that this offering is
inadequate, and that we deserve a £2 voucher each at the very least. If you agree,
please send this as 2 £2 vouchers. However, if you do not agree, we would like our £2
voucher returned in the format of 2 £1 vouchers, as due to our differing tastes in crisps
and recent disagreements over rhombi, we cannot bear to go shopping together.

Yours faithfully,

NICOLA JOY

KARINA EVANS

NICOLA JOY
KARINA EVANS

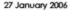

27 January 2006

Customer Services
Walkers Snack Food Ltd
PO Box
Leicester
LE4 8ZU

Ref: C/WK/05/12/3129/PC/55

Dear Sir/Madam

We wrote to you quite sometime ago regarding a complaint in relation to the shape of walkers square crisps. You sent us a measly two-pound voucher in response. We returned this to you asking for a larger offering. If this was declined we asked that our two pound voucher be returned to us in the format of two one pound vouchers as we no longer shop or share bags of crisps together. Our only other option would be tearing it in half and this, in our opinion, would render it useless. So the burning question, where are our new vouchers? We would appreciate it if you would inform us immediately as we want them to be in our possession as soon as possible. We sent the original voucher back enclosed safely in an envelope with a letter dated 26 November 2005. Our mathematician has calculated that we have been waiting an excruciating sixty-two days for the safe return of our vouchers, and quite frankly we think you are taking the piss.

We would like a full investigation into why this has taken so long to deal with and our voucher returned immediately in the required format. We would also like the postage cost of this letter refunded too.

Yours with irritation

NICOLA JOY

KARINA EVANS

**KARINA EVANS
NICOLA JOY**

6 December 2005

Hastings Borough Council
Parking Services
Century House
Menzies Road
East Sussex
TN38 9BB

Dear Sir/Madam,

Ourselves, our peers, and our ancestors have been using the parking services of Hastings for many many years, and have always found them to be pleasant places to leave our cars whilst we go about our daily business. Our views have changed somewhat since. purely by accident, stumbling across the car park in The Bourne, Old Town, Hastings. Our daily business is very limited on a Tuesday, and this particular day took us to the Old Town. We wished to park our car in a pleasant Hastings Borough Council car park for a maximum of half an hour whilst our daily business was being sorted out. Try as we might, we could not get the machine to let us park our car for half an hour. It appeared that the minimum time for parking was a whole hour, and nothing less. We eventually caved in and paid for a whole hour, whilst seething inside. In order to get value for money we ended up wandering in the rain for an extra 40 minutes after we had finished our daily business so that we did not waste our car parking fee. Our daily business regularly takes us to the Old Town these days, particularly on a Tuesday, and we are disturbed to discover that we are wasting several years of our lives wandering aimlessly around the picturesque, yet somewhat rainy, Old Town, Hastings, or alternatively wasting several hundreds of pounds on your stubborn, pay by the hour, ugly, stupid parking machine in The Bourne, Old Town, Hastings, East Sussex. We would appreciate a letter of explanation as soon as possible.

Yours,

KARINA EVANS

NICOLA JOY

Please quote: E&S/RS/ls
Your reference:
Date: 15 December 2005
Please ask for: Rasoul Shahilow
Telephone
Fax:
E-mail:

Hastings
BOROUGH COUNCIL
...Making the Difference...
Parking Services
Century House, 100 Menzies Road
St Leonards on Sea, East Sussex TN38 9BB
Tel: Fax:
email:

Hastings Borough Council
General enquiries:
email:
www.hastings.gov.uk
minicom:

Ms Karina Evans and Nicola Joy

Dear Ms Evans and Ms Joy
<u>Parking in the Old Town, Hastings</u>

Thank you for your letter dated 6 December and I am surprised to hear that you are of the opinion that one hour is excessive for the purpose of your parking in the Old Town.

The pricing tariff and times have been in place for well over twenty years and the Council has no intention of reducing the parking period times.

Pay and Display bays allow parking at half hour intervals and there are a number of bays just outside the Bourne Car Park. May I suggest you make use of this facility when visiting the Old Town in the future.

Yours sincerely,

Rasoul Shahilow
Parking Services Manager

KARINA EVANS
NICOLA JOY

28 December 2005

Parking Services
Century House
100 Menzies Road
St Leonards-on-Sea
East Sussex
TN38 9BB

Ref: E&S/RS/ls

Dear Mr Shahilow,

We reply with reference to the above. We thank you for your explanatory, although rather curt, reply to our original letter regarding the parking services in the Old Town of Hastings. Unfortunately, you do not seem to have solved our problem at all. When our daily business takes us to the Old Town on a Tuesday (which we *did* explain in great detail in our last letter), we do not want to be dragging our useless car around the Old Town in its entirety in a vain attempt to find a parking space in a bay that no-one else will dare attempt to get into, as it's inevitably too close to the double yellow lines/too close to the BMW in front/does not exist at all. Our point being that there are very rarely spaces in the parking bays, as many people go to the Old Town on their daily business on a Tuesday, and on the rare occasion that there are spaces, they are nigh on impossible to get in. If only we had a small compact car, like an Audi TT for example. If you purchased us one of these each, it would definitely make us feel better.

Please let us know if this is a feasible option to solve our parking nightmare,

Yours in anticipation,

KARINA EVANS

NICOLA JOY

Hastings

BOROUGH COUNCIL

...Making the Difference...

Parking Services
Century House, 100 Menzies Road
St Leonards on Sea, East Sussex TN38 9BB

Please quote:	E&S/RS/ls
Your reference:	
Date:	18 January 2006
Please ask for:	Rasoul Shahilow
Telephone	
Fax:	
E-mail:	

Hastings Borough Council
General enquiries:

www.hastings.gov.uk

Ms Karina Evans and Nicola Joy

Dear Ms Evans and Ms Joy

Old Town Parking

I am in receipt of your letter dated 28 December; received at this office on the 10 January.

Unfortunately there is not much more I can add to my previous answer to resolve your problem.

I am sorry you are unable to find an appropriate parking space in the Old Town every Tuesday but by the very nature of its name the Old Town is just that, old. The streets were never designed to take the present volume of traffic and parking. Indeed Preservation Societies want fewer parking spaces as they consider it makes the Old Town less attractive. Therefore you will appreciate the difficulties in trying to achieve an acceptable balance of adequate parking for residents, the business community and visitors.

With the high number of visitors attracted to the Old Town, especially in the Summer, it has become of victim of its own success.

I trust this answers your enquiry.

Yours sincerely,

Rasoul Shahilow
Parking Services Manager

NICOLA JOY
KARINA EVANS

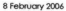

8 February 2006

Parking Services
Century House
100 Menzies Road
St Leonards on Sea
TN38 9BB

Ref: E&S/RS/ls

Dear Mr Shahilow,

With reference to the above reference and our recent correspondence with yourself.
We are concerned that you are not taking our concerns seriously, as you have
blatantly and cruelly ignored our requests for a small, easy to park car, such as an
Audi TT. After much consideration and deliberation we have thought of an idea that
will both preserve the attractiveness of the Old Town, *and* achieve an acceptable
balance of adequate parking for residents, the business community and visitors. A
discreet underground car park. This is more or less self-explanatory, and we are
concerned that it has not been considered before.

Although we appreciate that the Old Town is a beautiful area of Hastings, and its
authenticity would be preserved if less, not more, automobiles could be parked in it,
we are only human, and have to go about our daily business somewhere. Perhaps
the Old Town could be made larger? Just a suggestion.

Please could you contact us to let us know which of these options you are going to
consider, and whether or not you have the funding for an Audi TT apiece. We do not
particularly enjoy the aesthetics of other small vehicles such as Smart cars (although
we do appreciate their convenience, and amazing ability to park in even the
smallest of spaces).

We look forward to hearing from you soon,

Yours,

KARINA EVANS

NICOLA JOY

Please quote: E&S/RS/ls
Your reference:
Date: 14 February 2006
Please ask for: Rasoul Shahilow
Telephone
Fax:
E-mail:

Hastings

BOROUGH COUNCIL
...Making the Difference...

Parking Services
Century House, 100 Menzies Road
St Leonards on Sea, East Sussex TN38 9BB
Tel:
email:

Hastings Borough Council
General enquiries:
email:
www.hastings.gov.uk
minicom:

Ms Karina Evans and Nicola Joy

Dear Ms Evans and Ms Joy
Parking in the Old Town, Hastings

Thank you for your letter dated 7 February, the contents of which I note.

Unfortunately, there is nothing further I can add to my previous replies.

Kind regards,

Yours sincerely,

Rasoul Shahilow
Parking Services Manager

Karina Evans & Nicola Joy

Nestle Customer Service
PO Box 203
York
YO19 1XY

27 June 05

Dear Mr Rown Tree

The midget enjoys green fruit gums. Unfortunately he is now bedridden and only able to drink clear soup through a straw, using the tiny hole we drilled next to his left incisor for this very purpose. He has never had much strength in his tiny jaw. And your extra chewy, extra sticky, extra stupid fruit gum finished him off.

K evans
K Evans

N Joy

Karina Evans & Nicola Joy

Nestle Customer Services
PO Box 203
York
YO19 1XY

10/02/06

Dear Sir/Madam

We wrote to you a while back to inform you of the critical condition of our midget. We are very disturbed that you do not seem to care about the condition that was inflicted upon him by your fruit gums. Please find enclosed original letter we sent you dated 27 June 05 and an invoice for his health care.

Thank you, we look forward to hearing from you soon.

Yours sincerely

K Evans

N Joy

Invoice 01 for Nestle   10/02/06

Nicola Joy & Karina Evans

Health Care for the Midget

228 days @ 23.3 pence per day

Amount Due **£53.12** ₚ

Nestlé UK Ltd

YORK YO91 1XY

Telephone
Facsimile

Register with Nestlé for the latest
product news & special offers
www.nestle.co.uk

Karina Evans Nicola Joy

DIRECT LINE:

DATE:

DIRECT FAX:

1660301A   25 February 2006

Dear Karina Evans and Nicola Joy

Thank you for your recent letter advising us that you have not received a reply to your previous letter.

Please accept our apologies.

I am sorry to learn of your disappointment with your recent purchases and am concerned that you feel that there has been a deterioration in the quality of this product.

We hope this is not too disappointing a reply but hope that you will continue to enjoy our other products. Thank you once again for taking the trouble to contact us.

Yours sincerely

I S Douglas

IP Lynne Lawrie
Consumer Relations Executive
Consumer Services

Karina Evans & Nicola Joy

Nestle UK Ltd
York
YO91 1XY

29 February 2006

Dear Madam

Thank you for your reply dated 25 February 2006. Unfortunately we don't like it. Can you please send us one that refers to our midget; he is very offended. If you are refusing to pay his health care bill he would like a present.

Thank you for your time.

Yours truly

K Evans

N Joy

NICOLA JOY
KARINA EVANS

10 April 2006

Caroline Flint MP
Department of Health
Richmond House
79 Whitehall
SW1A 2NS

Dear Sir/Madam,

We are writing to you regarding a particular product that you allow to be manufactured, namely super strength lager. We truly believe this product to be the urine of Satan, and have been gathering evidence to prove this. So far we have obtained the following:

- 17 drunken 11-14 year olds
- 1 drunk baby
- 36 people with minor injuries
- 18 empty, discarded super strength lager cans
- 6 bald cats

This may well be a normal everyday occurrence in other towns, but this is one weekday night in the fine town of Hastings, by the sea. Although we have no conclusive proof that the cats were defuzzed by individuals under the influence of super strength lager, we did see several suspicious looking characters with cans and some rechargeable, cordless clippers.

We also have evidence to show that super strength lager breeds 'chavitis'. This came to light whilst we were returning home after our proof gathering. Upon entering the town centre of Hastings, by the sea, we noticed a group of young females, all in possession of cans of 'Devil Wee' (to give it its street name). The girls were having a little bit of an argument about the last king-size cigarette, when they suddenly flew at each other, wailing like banshees with their arms flailing like windmills. We truly believe that if these girls had been drinking an alternative alcoholic beverage then the disagreement would merely have resulted in the two girls 'going twos' on the last king-size cigarette.

We do not want to complain too much, as we are sure it can taste very pleasant under extreme circumstances. We would, however, like an explanation as to why you continue to allow such a product to be manufactured, when it is blatantly having such a hugely adverse effect on society and its youth.

Yours,

NICOLA JOY

KARINA EVANS

EXTREME CIRCUMSTANCES IN WHICH ONE WOULD WISH TO DRINK SUPER STRENGTH LAGER

1. If one's taste buds had been removed

2. If one was inconveniently situated up a mountain, with only the choice of slimy pond water or super strength lager to quench one's thirst

3. If one was blessed with an iron liver. One would certainly need one in order to stomach this crap

4. If one had been subjected to a life of ritual humiliation and taunting from all and sundry

5. If one had returned home after a night out, only to find one's cat in the unfortunate situation of having been reluctantly defuzzed

6. If one is in the regrettable predicament of having a gun held to one's head by an evil imp, and being forced to drink super strength lager or die

7. If one's Grandmother's face was so minging that one could not face looking at her without a sup

8. Similarly, if one's offspring were equally as minging as the above

(DH) Department of Health

Our ref: TO00000091591

Richmond House
79 Whitehall
London
SW1A 2NS

Tel:

Ms Nicola Joy and Ms Karina Evans

26 April 2006

Dear Ms Joy and Ms Evans,

Thank you for your letter of 10 April to the Department of Health about alcohol and 'super strength drinks'.

The Government recognise your concerns about the risks to health of those individuals who frequently drink hazardous or harmful quantities of very strong lagers and ciders, as well as the wider adverse social impacts that this causes. However, Government's ability to restrict the sale of such drinks is limited by EU Single Market legislation that provides for the free movement of goods and services and preventing obstacles to trade. As such, it would be difficult for the Government to prevent the sale of certain alcoholic drinks.

The Government therefore believe that it should deploy other mechanisms to seek to prevent alcohol-related harms. The Government has been working with the drinks and retail industries to develop a voluntary social responsibility scheme, as recommended in the *Alcohol Harm Reduction Strategy for England*. This work has included the development and publication of a national Principles and Standards document for producers and retailers which includes clear protocols around seeking proof of age, and ensuring that retailers have a clear policy of not selling alcohol to individuals who appear to be intoxicated, as well as putting disciplinary procedures in place to support this. The Government has impressed upon the industry the need for it to ensure effective take-up and implementation of the document, in order for it to have a real impact on the ground. The Government are also developing the National Producers Fund, working with both industry and non-industry stakeholders to develop the existing Drinkaware Trust (the charitable arm of The Portman Group) as the mechanism for delivering the Fund.

The Government is aware, from actions taken by other EU countries, that increasing the price of alcohol through the tax system can, at least in the short-term, reduce consumption levels, especially in younger drinkers. For the UK, as you know, tax issues are a matter for the Chancellor of the Exchequer.

The Government welcomes the industry's commitment in its *Principles and Standards* document, to place a sensible drinking message on packaging, advertising and at points of sale. Caroline Flint recently met with representatives of the alcohol industry

107

and asked that a small group be established to work with Department of Health officials, to develop a range of sensible drinking messages and unit information that can be displayed on alcoholic drinks labels and at the point of sale, as well as to look at preventing irresponsible alcoholic drinks promotions. The group has been asked to consider the standardisation of such messages, and that they report back to Ms Flint by the end of April.

I hope you find this reply helpful.

Yours sincerely

Kalpana Chauhan
Customer Service Centre
Department of Health

Nicola Joy
Karina Evans

Z.S.L.
London Zoo
Outer Circle
Regents Park
London
NW1 4RY

01/09/05

Dear Sir/Madam,

On a recent family day out to London Zoo with our child, we were most disturbed to discover that you do not keep your wasps in an enclosure. We are fully aware that we are not supposed to feed the animals/insects but we have a confession. We inadvertently fed a wasp when it sneakily descended upon our sweet sticky ice cream. Your zookeepers had obviously been neglecting it, as it was quite obviously suffering from malnourished. Once we had removed it from the ice cream it proceeded to follow us like a heat seeking missile, which scared us terribly and spoilt our family day out and ruined our communal ice cream. We sincerely hope that you will take measures in the future to prevent this from happening to other innocent day-trippers. We would appreciate it greatly if you could keep us informed on what you are planning to do about this serious issue.

Yours truly

Nicola Joy

Karina Evans

PATRON: H.M. THE QUEEN

The Zoological Society of London (ZSL) Founded in 1826 is headed Director
General and Council of a Council of 15 Fellows elected by and responsible to
the Fellowship

REGENT'S PARK LONDON NW1 4RY

www.zsl.org

Nicola Joy/Karina Evans

08 March 2006

Dear Nicola and Karina

Thank you for your communication, reported to me today.

I look forward to sending you a formal response as soon as possible. Please bear in
mind that we run a very busy department but aim to respond to all letters as we best
can.

Yours sincerely

A. Gould

Alix Gould
Education Administrator, ZSL

INSTITUTE OF ZOOLOGY
LONDON ZOO   WHIPSNADE WILD ANIMAL PARK
The Zoological Society of London is a registered charity. No: 208728

Nicola Joy
Karina Evans

Microsoft Limited
Microsoft Campus
Thames Valley Park
Reading
RG6 1WG

12/08/05

Dear Sir/Madam,

Whatever has possessed you? Not satisfied with animated inanimate office assistants, you have now transcended into a parallel universe with your stupid, stupid, smug, patronising, extra ugly, extra ginger, extra annoying cat that survives on little or no food.

Yes, we use the space bar a lot
Yes, we are trying to write a letter
Yes, we're trying to scroll long distances
No, we don't want our stars turned into bullet points.

Get your stupid, whiskered cat's nose out of our important documents, and leave us to our own long-winded methods. WE DON'T NEED YOUR CAT'S HELP.

We hate to think what horrors await us when we upgrade.

Yours faithfully,

NICOLA JOY

KARINA EVANS

Microsoft

Microsoft Limited
Microsoft Campus
Thames Valley Park
Reading RG6 1WG

Ms Nicola Joy and Ms Karina Evans

Reference: **SR 1-822394076**

Date: 07 March 2006

Dear Ms Joy and Ms Evans,

Office Assistant

Thank you for taking the time to provide this feedback to Microsoft® regarding our product.

I would like to assure you that we do consider such feedback to be extremely valuable as it helps us to improve the products and service that we offer. With this in mind I will make sure that your feedback is passed to the appropriate department for their consideration.

Have you considered disabling the Office Assistant? This can be done by right clicking on the Cat and choosing option, select. Then you deselect use the office assistant and then ok.

You can also hide the office assistant. Click on help and then choose hide the office assistant.

If we can be of any further assistance please contact us on 0870 60 10 100 Monday to Friday 8am - 6pm, e-mail us or visit www.microsoft.co.uk for all your information and support needs.

Yours sincerely,

Imtiaz Khan

Customer Service Professional
Microsoft Customer Services

Registered in England no. 1624297
VAT no GB 724 5946 15

And now for the ones that were *soooo* rude the

they couldn't be bothered to reply...

PEOPLE'S PIES

20 November 2003

Consumer Affairs
Philip Morris International
1001 Lausanne
Switzerland

Dear Mr Marlboro,

We recently happened upon a tobacconist and made a frivolous purchase, against our better judgement, of 2 large packets of Marlboro lights. We perused the warnings upon the box, and discussed, at great length, the implications upon our sperm. We realised that, being female, we have no sperm and therefore believed that smoking your cigarettes would be safe.

Imagine our horror, disgust and utter dismay when upon inhalation of aforementioned cigarette...we coughed. Just when we thought we were getting the hang of it, a large plume of mainline smoke hit us in the eye, thus making our eyes stingy and watery and ruining our eye make up. We were horrified, threw the box on the floor, stamped on it and promptly gave up smoking.

We are writing to you to suggest that you incorporate these events within the warnings on your boxes, thus ensuring other consumers do not frivolously waste good money on the aforementioned cigarettes. We have enclosed some suggestions on a separate sheet.

We look forward to hearing from you soon,

Yours with gay abandon and trauma,

Nicoli Joy

Karina Evans

<u>WARNING</u>

WARNING: Smoking will make your eyes stingy and watery, thus ruining your eye make up.

WARNING: Smoking will make your fingers smelly and turn them a disgusting shade of yellow.

WARNING: Smoking will yellow the teeth.

WARNING: Smoking will give you the breath of a thousand dogs.

WARNING: Smoking will make your legs look like corned beef.

WARNING: Smoking will make you thirsty.

WARNING: If cigarette packet is not closed correctly cigarettes will fall out.

WARNING: Cigarettes may leave a trail of straggly bits of tobacco in their wake.

WARNING: If cigarettes get wet they will not light properly.

WARNING: If hair is light blonde, cigarettes may turn it yellow.

WARNING: Too many cigarettes will make your voice gravelly in manner of a man.

WARNING: Do not light cigarettes in close vicinity of a gas leakage.

Karina Evans and Nicola Joy

Robert Dyas
Cleeve Court
Cleeve Road
Leatherhead
Surrey
KT22 7SD

01/07/05

Dear Robert Dyas,
With reference to an incident that occurred at approximately 10.57am on 03 May
2004. Do you mind if we call you Robbie? We cannot believe that you are a famous
singer, and meant to be an inspiration to leather clad middle aged women everywhere.
Yet you actively promote the activity of self-mutilation with your quite frankly
disgusting hand shredder.
Why??

Yours with three hundred and fifty two digits apiece flapping in the breeze

Karina Evans

Karina Evans

Nicola Joy

Nicola Joy

NICOLA JOY
KARINA EVANS

12 September 2005

Jim Boyce
Irish Football Association
20 Windsor Avenue
Belfast
BT9 6EE
Northern Ireland

Dear Mr Boyce,

We are writing regarding the England V Northern Ireland match that took place on 07/09/05. We were disturbed to note the visual distraction techniques employed by yourselves in order to sidetrack England's challenged footballers and ensure that Northern Ireland won the game.

The distractions in question were in the guise of bright, flashing, flickering, advertisements placed along the sides of the pitch. At one point, we saw Mr Rooney's eyes glaze over, in what can only be described as a stupor, as he stumbled haphazardly towards the malicious lights in question.

'Land of The Dead'

'Pride, Passion, Belief'

they cried selfishly.

We were so cross we blew our foghorns in outrage. Even Sven angrily pursed his lips.

Please can you reply as soon as possible to justify these heinous actions,

Yours angrily,

NICOLA JOY

KARINA EVANS

Sharky Shortbottom
Wilhelmina Longbottom

Ferrero U.K. Ltd
Awberry Court,
Watford
WD18 8RA

27/10/05

Dear Sir/Madam

We are writing with regard to Kinder Happy Hippo biscuit. And yes, we bet it is a very happy hippo with two large mammaries stuck upon its face in place of nostrils. We think that it is verging on soft porn. We are disgusted and disturbed that you market these as a children's sweet. At least cover them with a bra.

We look forward to receiving some sort of explanation from you shortly.

Yours with shock

The Shark

The Willy

Dr Evans/Dr Joy
Microbiological Suite/Disease Control Unit

The Bank of England
Thread Needle Street
London
EC2 R8AH

06/03/06

Dear Sir/Madam,

If our calculations are correct (which they usually are), taken from the common fact that each bowl of peanuts found in a typical pub contains seventeen different types of urine, we have concluded that each bank note contains;

75,352,021 different types of urine
128,942 different types of nasal mucus
35,296 different strengths of class A narcotics
100,000,027 different types of bacteria, viruses and the common cold
A lot of fingerprints
1 scattering of nasal hair complete with roots
1 really hideous picture of The Queen

Have you ever considered adding an anti bacterial agent before you start a pandemic of viruses?

Thank you for your time, we would very much like to know what you are going to do about this. Please find enclosed one sae for your speedy response.

Yours faithfully

Dr Joy

Dr Evans

Section 2

Because we don't complain all the

time

Gordon Bear-Bottom
Henrietta Bear-Bottom
Goggledybumpz

10 January 2004

Masterfoods
Leicestershire
LE14 4RS

Dear Sirs,

You are amazing. Just amazing. We have just eaten the best pie ever. We were holding a pre-Christmas dinner party when we stumbled upon an unforeseen obstacle. What should we eat? We wanted something a little exotic and so decided upon cat pie. We hear this is a delicacy in certain parts of the world. As we could not face the thought of butchering a cat ourselves, we ventured to our local supermarket. Can you imagine our surprise, delight and utter glee when we saw tins of ready butchered cat (Whiskas cat meat) in tins upon the shelves? We purchased a large quantity of these tins and raced home to make the largest cat pie in the world. It was delicious. Just delicious. All our guests are raving about it. We are thinking of trying dog or fox next time. Maybe you should branch out into the cat pie market so that everyone can enjoy the 'flava' and unique taste. We are willing to make cat pie for you for a small profit.

We look forward to hearing from you soon regarding this business venture,

Yours faithfully,

Gordon Bear-Bottom

Henrietta Bear-Bottom

A Division of Mars U.K. Limited
Freeby Lane
Waltham-on-the-Wolds
Melton Mowbray
Leicestershire LE14 4RS

Our Ref: 1291674A

Mr G Bear-Botton

2 January 2004

Dear Mr Bear-Botton

Thank you for your recent letter regarding the suitability of feeding cat food to humans.

Our pet foods are produced under hygienic conditions and cooked at temperatures which make the products sterile.

Whilst designed for animal palates, the products are perfectly safe should they be consumed by humans (e.g. accidentally by toddlers from a dog or cat bowl), so we can categorically reassure you that humans will not come to any harm through eating cat food. However, we should stress we would not recommend using cat food as a long-term feeding regime for a human.

As a member company of the Pet Foods Manufacturers' Association, we only use raw materials from animals which have been inspected and passed as fit for human consumption.

In addition, member companies only use raw materials from animal species which are generally recognised as accepted in the human food chain. This rules out the use of any materials from horses, ponies, cats, dogs, whales, other sea mammals or other species. It means that the industry only uses materials of beef, lamb, poultry and pork origin, fish, shellfish, rabbit.

Thank you for taking the time to contact us. If you need any further information or advice please contact our Consumer Careline on the telephone number below and one of our Consumer Care Advisors will be more than happy to help you.

Yours sincerely

Frances Lee
Consumer Care Advisor

T   , F   - www.mars.com

Registered at the Companies Registration Office: London, England · Registered number 636458 · Registered Office: 3d Dundee Road, Slough SL1 4LG
MASTERFOODS is a trademark

FOR HELP & ADVICE   Email:

**KARINA EVANS
NICOLI JOY**

7 March 2006

Bloomsbury Publishing Plc
36 Soho Square
London
W1D 3QY

Dear Sir/Madam,

As avid Harry Potter fans, myself and my good friend Nicoli were fidgeting with anticipation whilst packing our rucksacks for our life changing journey to Hogwarts. We set off to Paddington station with a spring in our step and glee in our eyes.

After having a good hunt around, on and off the tracks, we finally found what we believed to be Platform nine and three quarters, and launched ourselves headlong into the wall. Our only saving grace were the hard hats we were wearing. We were rendered slightly unconscious, and awoke to find ourselves being dragged away by armed police. Fear descended upon us, and we found ourselves shouting 'STOP THE BUS. We are not Brazilians, it's only our bikini lines'.

Please bear this in mind when you publish your next instruction book.

Can you please send us the real directions to Hogwarts.

Yours with anticipation,

KARINA EVANS

NICOLI JOY

Karina Evans & Nicola Joy

Fire Department City Of New York
9 Metrotech Centre
New York

06 December 2005

Dear Sir/Madam,

We are not sure if you've heard of a television programme entitled 'Jim'll Fix It', but he is somewhat of a national institution in our home country. Unfortunately, he did not fix it for us, so we are hoping that you can help.

It has always been our ambition to be rescued by New York fire-fighters. As burning buildings have a slight element of risk, we felt that it would be safer to be rescued from a big old oak tree (although we are not certain you have oak trees in America, but any tree will do). If it makes you feel better we will dress up as cats and miaow really loudly.

Can you please let us know as soon as possible when your fire-fighters are least busy and can carry out this rescue operation; we are travelling all the way from England and need to book our flights. We are happy to fit Operation Big Old Oak Tree around you, at your convenience. We will bring tea and scones in return for a guided tour around the fire station, and a ride upon your fire engine.

We have enclosed a self addressed envelope for your speedy response.

Thank you for your time, we look forward to hearing from you soon.

Yours in anticipation,

KARINA EVANS

NICOLA JOY

PS. Can you please tell us the location of the biggest oak tree in New York City so that we can practise climbing it in preparation for the big day.

PPS. Do your fire-fighters prefer rescuing tabbies or tortoiseshells? Or hedgehogs?

Karina Evans & Nicola Joy

15 February 2006

Fire Department of New York
9 Metrotech Centre
Brooklyn
New York
11201
U.S.A

Dear Sir/Madam

We wrote to you quite soon time ago in relation to dressing up as cats and being rescued from a tree by your firemen (please find copy of original letter enclosed). We have been waiting patiently for just over two months for a reply. We know that you have burning buildings etc etc to contend with but this is ridiculous. You don't even have an excuse not to reply as we sent you a self addressed envelope and an international reply coupon. We would like a reasonable explanation immediately or the return of our coupon.

Thank you for your time, stop wasting ours. We look forward to hearing from you soon.

Yours truly,

Karina Evans

Nicola Joy

NICOLA JOY & KARINA EVANS

07 September 2005

Michael Foster MP
The Ellen Draper Centre

Dear Michael Foster MP,

We understand that you are a very important man around town. A man of the night, shall we say? We are approaching you with a thoroughly decent proposal regarding the fake roundabout halfway up South Terrace. At present, it is nothing more than a useless circle on the floor. We can change this and rescue the fake roundabout to give it a purpose. We would like to place upon it a sign and/or friend with a sandwich board advertising our book in progress, 'We Are Disturbed'. We have a publisher, you know. This has not only the obvious benefit of free advertising, but will also give the fake roundabout some meaning to its existence. Please let us know your opinions on this matter as soon as possible, and give us some guidance on how to proceed with this proposal.

Yours truly,

NICOLA JOY

KARINA EVANS

MICHAEL FOSTER DL MP
Member of Parliament for Hastings and Rye

HOUSE OF COMMONS
LONDON SW1A 0AA

Karina Evans and Nicola Joy

Our Ref: AS/ 051636

14 September 2005

Dear Karina Evans and Nicola Joy

RE: Roundabout at South Terrace

Thank you for your letter received on the 9th of September. I was most intrigued to learn about your book in progress and your suggestions as to how it could be advertised.

Unfortunately this would seem to be an issue for the local Council and as your MP I would not therefore have any particular influence over what they might decide to allow.

I would suggest you make some initial enquiries with the Council as to your proposals (if you call _____ they will put you through to the appropriate department) and it would also be helpful for you to lobby your local Councillors and ask for their support.

Best wishes

Yours sincerely

MICHAEL FOSTER DL MP

NICOLI JOY
KARINA EVANS

13 January 2006

Nationwide Building Society
Head Office
Nationwide House
Pipers Way
Swindon
Wiltshire
SN38 1NW

Dear Sir/Madam,

We have watched your recent advertising campaign with growing interest and a sense of joy. Your most recent advertisement implies that regardless of how you look, your loan rate will be the same as everyone else's, unlike other money lenders.

The reason we are contacting you is because as two extraordinarily good looking people, we would like you to put us in contact with the money lenders who base their loan rate on looks alone. We know that we are beautiful and we do not agree that beautiful and ugly people are equal in today's society. We feel very strongly that the more aesthetically pleasing one is, the more money one should be able to get.

Thank you for raising such a valid point in your commercial.

We look forward to hearing from you soon,

Yours,

NICOLI JOY

KARINA EVANS

Dick Soar-Botomme
Kat O'Neine

28 April 2006

Superdrug Stores Plc
Admail 838
Croydon
UK
CR9 4WZ

Dear Friend,

We are great fans of your range of products, particularly your rubber gloves, we wear them often for various activities. However, we are beginning to find the design quite wearisome, and the colours are, quite frankly, crude and tawdry.

May we suggest, when you next conduct a product evaluation, that you consider designing the gloves to be less yielding, as currently they allow a little too much movement, and occasionally fluid shrewdly finds its way into the interior part of the glove, moistening our fingers and attached hands. As you can imagine, this is undesirable, particularly in our line of work.

May we also make some suggestions with reference to the colour of the gloves. We find the colours a little too garish, and would like to suggest that a gleaming black glove would be a little more appealing and less visible in a darkened room.

Sincerely,

D Soar-Bottomme

K O'Neine

03/05/06

Mr Soar -botomme

Reference: PM328148

Superdrug Stores plc
A member of the A.S. Watson Group

118 Beddington Lane
Croydon
Surrey CR0 4TB
United Kingdom
Tel
Fax

Dear Mr Soar-Botomme and Ms Kat O'Neine,

Thank you for your recent letter regarding Superdrug rubber gloves.

We always appreciate feedback from our customers as we are continually striving to improve the quality of our products and, therefore, our customer satisfaction.

I was happy to hear that you are great fans of our products especially our gloves. Your comments regarding the gloves have been noted and I have spoken to our Buyer for the household section in relation to this. They inform me that they are currently looking at various exciting different ranges which should be in our shops very soon.

In the meantime I have enclosed two samples of gloves for you to try with our compliments, both of which you may find suitable for your uses. The disposable gloves are highly sensitive latex and have the added benefit of being disposable after use and the sensitive gloves have a long cuff which is useful to prevent fluids finding its way into the interior part of the glove.

Thank you for taking the time to write to us and I hope we can continue to be of service to you in the future.

Yours sincerely,

CUSTOMER RELATIONS DEPARTMENT

Health & Beauty from A.S. Watson

NICOLA JOY
KARINA EVANS

09 March 2006

Consumer Relations Department – UK
Cadbury Trebor Bassett
PO Box 12
Bournville Lane
Bournville
Birmingham
B30 2LU

Dear Sir/Madam,

We have always been of the impression that Bertie Bassett is a character developed by yourselves for the purpose of selling oodles of liquorice allsorts. Our worlds were turned upside down recently due to an unexpected sighting of him outside our kitchen window. This was at approximately the same time that we saw an alien. Are these two sightings linked? We hope that you hold the answer to this puzzle.

Please can you write back to us immediately as we need to forward our findings to the Queen.

Yours with unease,

NICOLA JOY

KARINA EVANS

TREBOR BASSETT

TREBOR BASSETT LTD

FREEPOST MID 20061
BIRMINGHAM B30 2QZ
TELEPHONE
FACSIMILE

17 March 2006

Ms N Joy & Ms Evans

Our Ref:- 1246613A

Dear Nicola and Karina,

Thank you for your recent letter which has been passed to me for response.

I was very concerned to learn of your recent experience. As far as we are aware Bertie is still in the confines of the factory where we produce Bassetts Liquorice Allsorts. He doesn't leave the factory very often as it is his job to oversee the production of his favourite sweets. From the information you have given it sounds like you may have come across an imposter who is trying to impersonate Bertie.

We have made Bertie aware of this sighting and he assures us that he is the one and only Bertie and has asked me to send you a voucher to purchase some Liquorice Allsorts with his very best wishes.

Thank you for taking the time to write to us.

Yours sincerely

Sarah Welch
Consumer Relations Department

Karina Evans & Nicola Joy

Richard Branson
Virgin Management Ltd
120 Campden Hill Road
London
W8 7AR

24/02/06

Dear Mr Branson,

You disappoint us; upon making a cheese and pickle sandwich we discovered your dark secret. Branson pickle was first made in 1922, yet you tell the public that you are currently 55 years of age. You have been rumbled, our mathematician has calculated that you must be at least 99 years of age. But do not fear, we are willing to you're your secret in exchange for a free ride in a hot air balloon.

We look forward to hearing from you soon, you naughty rascal.

Karina Evans

Nicola Joy

PS Can you please forward us the number of your plastic surgeon?

BILL & BEN FLOBADOBALOBADOS

21 February 2006

Schweppes
Coca-Cola Enterprises Limited
Uxbridge
UB8 1EZ

Dear Sir/Madam,

As you are a giant soft drinks manufacturer, we are hoping that you can help us with a query regarding the different types of lemonade.

We have encountered the original version, and also a 'Diet' form of the same product. Our concerns stem from warnings about the negative side effects of both of these products.

We have found ourselves in the unfortunate position of being stuck between a rock and a hard place when we have a attempted to purchase either of these products. Do we buy the original version, which will undoubtedly render us obese? Or, alternatively, do we purchase the 'Diet' variety, which contains carcinogenic sugar substitutes, and will perhaps riddle us with tumours?

We would really appreciate your views on this matter, as we are stuck with a huge bottle of Advocaat, and no mixer.

Thank you for your time,

BILL & BEN FLOBADOBALOBADOS

Date - 23 March 2006

Mr Bill & Ben Flobadobalobados

Great Britain
1 Queen Caroline Street
Hammersmith London W6 9HQ
Tel   Fax

Our ref: 06/03/154846

Dear Mr Flobadobalobados,

Thank you for your recent letter to the 'Coca-Cola' Consumer Information Centre.

A balanced diet includes a variety of foods, and as long as someone eats a balanced diet, any food, including a soft drink, is acceptable. Soft drinks are also an enjoyable way of contributing to the daily fluid intake which the human body needs. There are no good or bad foods, only good or bad diets.

Coca-Cola Great Britain offers consumers a wide range of beverages, both with sugar and sugar free options. It is at the consumers discretion, which products they choose to consume.

I would like to thank you for taking the time to contact us and for your interest in our company and our brands.

Yours sincerely,

Karen Leu
Consumer Information Centre
Coca-Cola Great Britain

Beverage Services Limited Incorporated in England No. 2072595
Registered Office: 1 Queen Caroline Street, London W6 9HQ
VAT No. 677 354 767

Nicola Joy
Karina Evans

Maritime & Coastguard Agency
Spring Place
105 Commercial Road
Southampton
SO15 1EG

20/09/05

Dear Sir/Madam

We are writing to you with regard to a long held dream concerning a helicopter and us flailing helplessly in the sea. We have been a little perturbed ever since the rejection of a certain Sir Jimmy Saville who failed to fix it for us fourteen years ago. We feel that this is our final shot at a grade A rescue mission and would therefore like to give you the opportunity to make our biggest dream come true*. We are willing to put ourselves forward to be pretend victims on one of your staff training days/pretend rescue mission days when you use your helicopter, you are more than welcome to airlift us from the sea, from the side of a cliff or pluck us off the back of a giant sea turtle; we're not fussy.

We are willing to make a small donation to the coastguard for this unique experience, we would make a large one but we are not plump of pocket at present.

We look forward to hearing from you soon.

Yours with gratitude and anticipation.

Nicola Joy

Karina Evans

*Excluding debauchery and decadence with certain A list actors

Maritime and Coastguard Agency

An executive agency of the Department for Transport

Andrew Burton
Bay 1/07
Spring Place
105 Commercial Road
Southampton
SO15 1EG
United Kingdom

Tel:
DDI:

Fax:
E-mail:

Nicola Joy & Karina Evans

04 October 2005

Dear Nicola and Karina,

Many thanks for your letter requesting to be "victims" in one of our Search and Rescue helicopter training sorties. Unfortunately, due to insurance and Civil Aviation Authority restrictions, I'm afraid (like Sir Jimmy) I am unable to accept your offer*.

Sincerely,

Andy Burton
Deputy Aviation Manager
Search and Rescue Brach

*I'm afraid that we don't have any A list actors on the books, either.

Nicola Joy & Karina Evans

Andrew Burton
Maritime & Coastguard Agency
Spring Place
105 Commercial Road
Southampton
SO15 1EG

Dear Andrew,

We are not amused at being rejected yet again, what is wrong with us? Why will nobody let us go in their helicopters? IT'S NOT FAIR! We are stamping in the manner of two year olds as we write this. However, we have a new proposal; if we have an orgy with you instead of A list actors then will you wangle us a ride in the coastguard helicopter? This is your last chance; if you do not comply we are going to approach the R.A.F.

Yours with renewed gratitude and anticipation,

Nicola Joy

Karina Evans

PS Please find enclosed copies of previous correspondence just in case you have forgotten who we are. We are great.

PPS Please return the attached paperclip, it's lucky.

Karina Evans & Nicola Joy

Headquarters Strike Command
R.A.F High Wycombe
Buckinghamshire
HP14 4UE

24 January 06

Dear Sir/Madam

We are writing in hope that someone in the Royal Air Force will be kind enough to
take us for a spin in a huge helicopter. We have asked Jim'll fix it, we have even
asked the coastguard, but oh no, they have both cruelly rejected us. : (

We feel that our lives are incomplete and only a ride in a helicopter will remedy this.
Please, please, please give us meaning in our lives and put a spring back in our steps
by flying us high in the sky. You are our last port of call.

HELP

Thank you for your time, we look forward to hearing from you soon.

Yours truly

Karina Evans

Nicola Joy

Sharky Shortbottom
Wilhelmina Longbottom
Gleely Botanics

30/03/06

M&S PLC
PO Box 3339
Chester
CH99 9QS

Dear Sir/Madam

We are writing to you in hope that you may consider stocking our genetically modified hybrid Cacti, aimed at the minimalist.

The invisible Cactus is so minimalist that it can't actually be seen; although when it flowers it does give of a very fragrant vanilla aroma. It will make a very pleasant addition to any abode.

We expect the Cacti to retail at around £4.99 each. We would like to send you a couple of specimens free of charge on a trial period, so you can experience first hand how amazing these plants are. If you would like to receive some we can forward some samples to your office very shortly. We do hope that you will consider these unique plants for your shelves.

Thank you for your time. We look forward to hearing from you soon.

Yours faithfully

Sharky Shortbottom

Wilhelmina Longbottom

**MARKS &
SPENCER**

Retail Customer Services
Chester Business Park
Wrexham Road
Chester
CH4 9GA
Tel:
Fax:
www.marksandspencer.com

Mr S Shortbottom

Our Ref: 1-104650656
4 April, 2006

Dear Mr Shortbottom

Thank you for your recent letter regarding the hybrid cacti aimed at minimalist living.

I have passed on your comments to our horticultural department and I am sure that they will contact you if they are interested in your invisible cacti.

Yours sincerely

J. Peck

Jackie Peck
Customer Adviser
Retail Customer Services

Marks and Spencer plc
Registered Office:
Waterside House
35 North Wharf Road
London W2 1NW
Registered No. 214436
(England and Wales)

The Shark & The Willy

18/05/06

Merrydown PLC
Castle Court
41 London Road
Reigate
Surrey
RH2 9RJ

Dear Sir/Madam

We are writing in hope that you will be able to help us. We recently heard on the grapevine that if you leave cider in a cupboard under a very strong lamp, say in the manner of growing weed, that in six weeks and one day it would have sprouted purple mushrooms. We don't want to try this ourselves, as we are afraid that it may not be legal. Would you please, please tell us if this is true and if so are the mushrooms harmful if consumed or in any way hallucinogenic? We would also like to know if this mushroom growing activity is legal.

Thank you for your time, we look forward to hearing from you soon.

Yours truly

The Shark

The Willy

MERRYDOWN®

PREMIUM CIDER & JUICE BRANDS

Ref: 6-112 cm Shark-Willy

15th June 2006

Messrs Shark and Willy

Without prejudice

Dear Shark and Willy

Please accept my apology for the delay in replying to your letter of enquiry.

We have utilised the intervening period to test out your assumptions and although the four lamps we used were each 150 watts we have been unable to get any mushrooms of any colour, let alone purple, to sprout..

As we were able to carry out these experiments under laboratory controlled conditions it was entirely legal for us, but probably not for Elasmobranchii nor male human appendages such as yourselves.

Should you wish to embark on your own investigations into such phenomena then we are pleased to enclose a voucher to enable you to purchase some Vintage cider which I trust you will find to be satisfactory. Please ask a responsible adult to make the purchase for you.

Yours sincerely
for Merrydown plc

Philip Baines
Customer Liaison

No-liability is admitted or implied by the action of this voucher that is presented solely as a gesture of goodwill on behalf of Merrydown plc.

MERRYDOWN PLC. CASTLE COURT, 41 LONDON ROAD, REIGATE, SURREY RH2 9RJ
T: F: web: www.merrydownplc.com
Registered in England No. 424215 Registered office: 110 Cannon Street, London EC4N 6AR

DREW PEACOCK
HAIRIE BASTARDE

Colin Farrell
Creative Artists Agency
9830 Wilshire Blvd
Beverly Hills CA 90212
USA

Dear Colin,

Our associates, the midget and the gimp have
developed a very unhealthy interest in you. They
have been shouting from the rooftops that they love
you, and now they think that they can fly. Would you
please come round and talk some sense into them?

Yours with a lot of concern,

D PEACOCK

H BASTARDE

Sharky Shortbottom
Wilhelmina Longbottom

15 February 2006

Richmond Sausages
Thorpe Lea Manor
Thorpe Lea Road
Egham
Surrey
TW20 8HY

Dear Sir/Madam

We are writing to you because we believe that we invented the word sausage. During a recent session of past life regression, we were transported back to the year 1623 BC. We were standing there with sandy toes, smoking cigars, in our loin cloths, on a yellow cobbled street when we saw a strange brown object being nibbled by a donkey. This is a transcript of the fateful conversation that gave sausages their name:

'By heck, George what is that strange thing? It looks like a sausage'
'A sausage? What's a sausage?'
'I don't know George, I just made it up'

A passing jester overheard our conversation and tried to steal our new word but we found him, silenced him and stole it back. We have now reached the inevitable conclusion that you have, like the evil jester, also stolen our word.

We appreciate that as you have established yourselves by using this word, it would be very difficult to give it back. We are willing to compromise; we will let you keep it if you make us up a new word, and give us credit on your packaging.

Yours,

'THE SHARK'

'THE WILLY'

'Sharky' Shortbottom
Wilhelmina Longbottom
Bottoms Down

08 February 2006

Heinz
South Building
Hayes Park
UB4 8AL

Dear Consumer Feedback,

Last Tuesday, we perused a container of the product entitled 'Heinz
Forest Mushroom Soup'. It was in the 'short date' bin in a local
respectable high street shop. Upon reading the label, a chill descended
upon us as it became clear that Heinz, the most respected soupers of all
time, were lying to us. Either that or we live in an Enid Blyton book. Our
concerns stem from the aforementioned 'Heinz Forest Mushroom Soup'.
We find it nigh on impossible to believe that you employ people solely
for forest mushroom picking, as this is back breaking work in a damp
environment and probably a major health and safety issue. If this is the
case then how on earth do they distinguish between bona fide souping
mushrooms, and their evil cousins of the 'magic' variety? Which forest
do they come from? If you cannot answer these questions satisfactorily,
then we shall continue with our assumption that the mushrooms are
standard supermarket fungi, or that, more believably, you have a gang
of elves in a forest picking mushrooms all day for little pay and no
thanks. That's cruel.

We look forward to your satisfactory explanation.

Yours in anticipation,

'THE SHARK'

'THE WILLY'

H. J. Heinz Company Limited

South Building, Hayes Park, Hayes, Middlesex UB4 8AL
Telephone: Care Line:
Internet: www.heinz.co.uk

001014375A

13 February 2006

Ms S Shortbottom

Dear Ms Shortbottom

We acknowledge your recent communication concerning our Forest Mushroom Soup Cup.

We note your comments and can assure you that our Research, Packaging and Design Department will be informed of your views.

Thank you for taking the trouble to contact us on the matter and trust you will accept the enclosed to obtain a complimentary pack.

Yours sincerely

Geoff Kearsley
Consumer Care Co-ordinator

For information
about Heinz
write to the above
address or visit
our website

www.heinz.co.uk

TO THE CUSTOMER: This voucher may be used as payment or part payment towards your grocery shopping bill to the value shown provided that at least one Heinz product is included amongst your purchases. It may not be redeemed for cash and NO change will be given if the voucher is tendered for items less than its full value. Heinz reserves the right not to accept damaged or defaced vouchers.
TO THE RETAILER: This voucher will be redeemed at its face value provided ONLY that it has been taken in payment or part payment towards grocery shopping that included at least one Heinz product. H.J. Heinz Co. Ltd. reserve the right to refuse payment against misredeemed, damaged or defaced vouchers. Vouchers must be submitted within six months of the voucher's validity date. Please submit to Heinz Coupon Redemption, PO Box 504, Leicester LE5H 0AE.

HEINZ

VOUCHER   VALID UNTIL LAST DAY OF   MAY06

'Sharky' Shortbottom
Wilhelmina Longbottom
Bottoms Down

21 February 2006

Heinz
South Building
Hayes Park
UB4 8AL

Ref: 00/014375A

Dear Heinz,

We are writing with reference to the above. We are slightly incensed by your reply, and note your comments which have frustrated us immensely.

We are angered that you have blatantly ignored our questions regarding the origins of the mushrooms placed in 'Forest Mushroom Soup'. We are presuming that your lack of explanation regarding the exploitation of the working elves is an admission of guilt. Elves are on the earth to be loved and cherished, if we exploit them for our own, evil mushroom picking needs we send a very negative message to the children of today. We suggest that these children are perhaps better suited to the mushroom picking than the elves. They generally have a better pincer grip.

We appreciate the hush money voucher that you forwarded to us, but I am afraid we cannot take it. Firstly, hush money should be in the form of cold, hard cash. Secondly, we reiterate the point that elves should not be exploited, nor their nimble fingers used, for the purpose of mushroom picking. For this reason we are returning your hush money. We expect an adequate explanation by return of post.

Yours,

'SHARKY'

'WILLY'

Randy Pansie
Joe Smith

13/3/2006

Sealife Centre
Marine Parade
Brighton
West Sussex
BN2 1TB

Dear Folk at the Sea life Centre,

We are adrenaline junkies and are always looking for our next thrill. It has come to our attention that diving with Great White Sharks in South Africa is becoming increasingly popular. We squeal with zeal at the thought of this but unfortunately cannot afford the airfare to fulfil our dreams. This is why we are writing to you, we are hoping that you are kind enough to grant us one small request; to let us come and dive with the Sharks in your Aquarium instead. We know that your sharks are not as big as Great Whites, but we are pretty sure that they will get our adrenaline pumping. We are very discreet and always wear camouflage wet suits so as not to startle anyone, including sharks. We would like to point out that we would preferably like to swim with them just after they have been fed. We like our limbs as they are; intact.

We would appreciate if you could let us know as soon as possible if it is likely that we can carry out the above exercise. Please forward us the most suitable dates for this.

Thank you for your time we look forward to hearing from you soon

Yours with excitement

R Pansie

J Smith

Randie Pansie
Joe Smith

13th March 2006

Dear Mr Pansie and Mr Smith

Re: Swimming with Sharks

Thank you for your enquiry regarding getting an adrenaline kick by swimming
with our sharks. In order to minimise any stress to these animals we strictly limit
the number of divers in our shark display to as few as possible – e.g. to administer
treatments and clean the display. We are therefore unable to invite you to swim
with sharks at the Sea-Life Centre.

I believe the Blue Reef Aquarium at Portsmouth allows people to swim with their
sharks providing they are doing so to raise money for charity, so you may have
more luck approaching them.

Once again I would like to thank you for your enquiry, and wish you luck in your
pursuit of adrenaline.

Regards

Rosie Adams
Customer Services

NICOLA JOY & KARINA EVANS

16 February 2006

Collins Word Exchange
77-85 Fulham Palace Road
London

Dear Friend,

We are currently in the process of scrutinising the Collins Compact English Dictionary (New Edition 1998 ISBN 0 00 472116 0), in a concerted effort to increase our limited vocabulary which will enable us to have pseudo-intelligent discussions with our elders. Unfortunately, we have come to an untimely and frustrating halt at the word 'lemming'. Although we know that we are slightly behind the times with our humble 1998 New Edition, and that the definition may well have since been updated, we feel that the current description is a little vague and perhaps a tad too tactful. The definition of the aforementioned word is as follows:

lemming *n* **1** a small rodent of northern and arctic regions, reputed to rush into the sea in large groups and drown. **2** a member of any group following an unthinking course towards destruction [Norwegian]

We feel that definition **1** needs to be reworded slightly in order to encompass the extraordinary foolishness of these ridiculous little creatures. Perhaps something similar to the following will suffice:

lemming *n* **1** a small, rather stupid, rodent of northern and arctic regions, reputed to rush into the sea in large, ridiculous groups and foolishly drown. **2** a member of any group following an unthinking course towards destruction [Norwegian]

We are sure that you can understand our frustration, particularly at this pivotal point in our self-education and improvement. Our minds are disturbed and we are currently incapable of participating in any discussions beginning with letters post L. This is particularly difficult when our elders attempt to involve us in a discussion about the war or x-ray machinery.

We look forward to your reply and thank you for your time,

Yours sincerely,

NICOLA JOY

KARINA EVANS

NICOLA JOY
KARINA EVANS

Hastings Borough Council
Town Hall
Queens Road
HASTINGS
East Sussex
TN34 1QR

02 November 2005

Dear Sir/Madam,

We recently contacted our local MP, Mr Michael Foster, regarding a proposal we have for a defunct roundabout in South Terrace. Please find enclosed a copy of the original letter. Mr Foster has kindly suggested that we contact yourselves with our proposal as you hold more decision making powers than him.

As we are sure you are aware, halfway up South Terrace there is a tiny, useless, lonely circle in the road. We are disturbed that such an important circle could be left on its own, with no purpose or life whatsoever. We propose that this circle is promoted to a roundabout, and that we could advertise our forthcoming book on it via the medium of signage and friends wearing sandwich boards.

Please can you contact us as soon as possible with directions on how to proceed with this.

Yours,

NICOLA JOY

KARINA EVANS

Transport and Environment

Robert E Wilkins
MSc CEng MICE MInstWM MIHT
Director

Derek Ireland FIHIE IEng
Highway Manager
Hastings Area

Century House
100 Menzies Road
St Leonards on Sea
East Sussex
TN38 9BB

Telephone Hastings

Fax

East Sussex County Council

Ms Nicola Joy
Ms Karina Evans

date
16 November 2005
your ref

when responding please contact
Peter Phillips
Telephone

our ref
C/T/V/PP/JN

Dear Ms Joy & Ms Evans

ROAD MARKINGS IN SOUTH TERRACE HASTINGS.

I refer to your letter dated 2 November 2005 requesting a change of use of road markings.

The white painted area of road can clearly be seen as part of an old traffic island. Unfortunately the island was demolished several times by goods vehicles possibly turning from Devonshire Road. It was decided on the last occasion not to reinstate it. The use to which you suggest may be colourful and brighten the road, but cannot be permitted or condoned. If any resurfacing is carried out in the vicinity it will be removed and the ghost island repainted.

Should you wish to discuss this or any other matter, I can be contacted on the telephone number shown above.

Yours sincerely

**D W IRELAND
HIGHWAY MANAGER**

X:\MS Word\Julie\Traffic\JoyEvansSthTerr.doc

Hastings
BOROUGH COUNCIL

Hastings Borough Council
Highway Management Contractor
to East Sussex County Council

153

NICOLA JOY
KARINA EVANS

7 February 2006

Hastings Borough Council
Town Hall
Queens Road
Hastings
TN34 1QR

Dear Sir/Madam,

We are writing with reference to a letter we sent you in November 2005 (please find copy enclosed). The letter outlined the fears we had for a small defunct roundabout halfway up South Terrace.

It has recently been brought to our attention that the road has since been heightened by approximately 1/8th of an inch. Firstly, we are writing to inform you that this work is overdue, for years we have been concerned about the difference in height between the road and the adjacent pavement. Heightening the road by 1/8th of an inch makes the journey across South Terrace less dangerous and infinitely more enjoyable. We thank you for this.

Secondly, we have noticed that during this recent work, the small, defunct roundabout halfway up South Terrace has consequently been covered over. We are delighted that you listened to our concerns about the roundabout and its lack of quality of life, but we are not great fans of live burials. We feel that the roundabout could have been put to a better use. You did not have to kill it.

We would like to know whether the roundabout is now going to be replaced with a younger, more modern version, or if this burial marks the beginning of a roundabout-free South Terrace.

We are also concerned that the council did not heed our advice in previous letters we sent last year about a separate incident. These letters highlighted the benefits of employing aesthetically pleasing workmen. Unfortunately, most of them look like Ron Jeremy. It is like walking onto an 80s porn set every morning.

We look forward to hearing from you soon,

Yours faithfully,

NICOLA JOY

KARINA EVANS

KARINA EVANS & NICOLA JOY

22 April 2006

Michael Foster MP

Dear Michael Foster MP,

We have not heard from you for a while, we do hope that everything is all right at your end. Our book is coming along nicely, thank you. Unfortunately, Hastings Borough Council did not grant us permission to advertise said book on defunct roundabout in South Terrace, with or without sandwich boards. The aforementioned roundabout has since been buried. Coincidence? Perhaps you could shed some light on this.

We have recently written to Tony Blair on several occasions but unfortunately he has had neither the courtesy nor time to reply. We are slightly miffed as these letters all contained bona fide queries and suggestions. Perhaps you could also help us with this? We would be extremely grateful if you could put in a good word for us, and forward us some tips on how to get replies. We would also like to know how one should behave around the Prime Minister, as if he invites us for coffee we do not wish to embarrass ourselves.

Thank you very much for you time, we wait in anticipation for your reply,

Yours,

KARINA EVANS

NICOLA JOY

MICHAEL FOSTER DL MP
Member of Parliament for Hastings and Rye

HOUSE OF COMMONS
LONDON SW1A 0AA

Karina Evans and Nicola Joy

Our Ref: MF/AS/01051636

25 April 2006

Dear Karina Evans and Nicola Joy

RE: Issues of Concern

Thank you for your letters of the 22 April. I am sorry that the Council felt unable to support your "advertising campaign" but I guess they probably received lots of similar requests.

Regarding your letter to the Prime Minister I can tell you his office receives some thousands of letters each day. That's why under the Parliamentary system although some will get acknowledgements they are usually passed on to the local MPs who are if you like the "local agent". MPs are then requested to either answer the letters or if they are something which need Minister responses they then are filtered and sent to Ministers for that purpose.

It would as I am sure you realise be impossible for the Prime Minister himself to deal with 60million constituents.

Do therefore please send me copies of any queries you have raised and I would be happy to try and answer them as your representative.

With best wishes,

Yours sincerely

MICHAEL FOSTER DL MP

Constituency Office:
Telephone:
MINICOM AVAILABLE Fax: Hastings
E mail: mp@1066.net

KARINA EVANS & NICOLA JOY

20 May 2006

Michael Foster MP

Dear Michael Foster MP,

Thank you for your letter inviting us to forward you the questions that the Prime Minister and his minions have refused to answer. We are very grateful that you are going to answer them for us. We feel that this is the most appropriate course of action as stalking the above important people is inadvisable.

The queries are as follows:

- Do aliens exist? We saw on at 7.41pm on a Tuesday evening at approximately the same time that we saw a pseudo Bertie Bassett (Trebor Bassett have since informed us that he was guarding the factory at the time).
- We have a format for a new snuff reality television show. Would it please be possible for the Government to donate us some 'lifers', as many as you can spare, so we can blow up, shoot, poison, maim and stab them on live television (preferably Channel 4). We did invite Charles Clarke to do this. He did not reply, but we believe that he did indeed send us some and they escaped. This is why he has been sacked. This time we need an approximate date for despatch so we can prepare our secure containers and executioners.
- How shall we behave when the Prime Minister/Queen invites us for tea? This is inevitable as we will surely be awarded lots of medals and a certificate for our dedicated disposal of Evil.

Thank you so much Michael. Your efforts will be noted and rewarded with a small gift as a token of our appreciation sometime in the distant future.

Yours,

KARINA EVANS

NICOLA JOY

MICHAEL FOSTER DL MP
Member of Parliament for Hastings and Rye

HOUSE OF COMMONS
LONDON SW1A 0AA

Karina Evans and Nicola Joy

Our Ref: JM/01051636

02 August 2006

Dear Karina Evans and Nicola Joy

RE: VARIOUS CONCERNS

Thank you for your letter dated the 20th of May, received on the 30th of June. I apologise for the delay in responding.

Unfortunately I don't have the answers to the questions you ask. I find 'google' is maybe the best source for such far reaching enquiries. I am sorry that I am unable to be of greater assistance.

Yours sincerely

MICHAEL FOSTER MP

Gordon & Henrietta Bear-Bottom

08 February 2006

The Natural History Museum
Cromwell Road
London
SW7 5BD

Dear Sir/Madam

Ourselves and our associates recently visited The Natural History Museum. We were amazed at the freakish sights that greeted us in the Darwin centre; the jarred specimens astounded us. As avid fans of obscure body parts and life forms we are hoping to add to our growing collection. We were wondering if you would like to make a donation. These highly unusual ornaments look great scattered around our dwelling, and are always a wonderful talking point at our dinner parties. We are very keen to expand our collection and if you cannot donate us any we are willing to purchase them.

Thank you for your time, we will hear from you soon.

Yours faithfully

G Bear-Bottom

H Bear-Bottom

Department of Zoology

Gordon & Henrietta Bear-Bottom

5 April 2006

Dear Gordon and Henrietta,

Thank you for your recent letter, apologies for the delay in replying. I am glad you enjoyed your visit to the Darwin Centre. Apart from the specimens that are on show to the public, the preserved organisms in our collections are used first and foremost as a scientific reference for researchers to examine. So unfortunately, Museum specimens cannot be given away or sold by us unless there is a very good, usually scientific, reason to do so, such as part of a formal exchange between institutions.

You sound as if you have a very interesting hobby, I hope that you would be abiding by the requisite legal regulations related to the possession of such material. I am pleased in any case that the diversity and strangeness of the natural world has given you such enjoyment and inspiration.

Yours sincerely,

Andrew Cabrinovic
Zoology Enquiries
Darwin Centre floor 5
The Natural History Museum
Cromwell Road
LONDON SW7 5BD
U.K.

Tel :
Fax :
Email :
Web : http://www.nhm.ac.uk//

The Natural History Museum Cromwell Road London SW7 5BD United Kingdom +44 (0)20 7942 5000 www.nhm.ac.uk

GAYE SALAMANDER
ROBERTO HANGADOLOFOSTI

7 March 2006

BUPA Hospitals
15-19 Bloomsbury Way
London
WC1A 2BA

Dear Sir/Madam,

We are writing with concern for our health. We recently read that psychopaths have lesions on their cortex. We are concerned and would like our own brains checked out. If we joined your medical plan, would it be possible to have some sort of head endoscopies done to put our minds at rest? If so, how much would this cost?

Yours truly,

G SALAMANDER

R HANGADOLOFOSTI

Nikkolla Joyye
Kerreina Evenns
Word Investigators

8 February 2006

Oxford University Press
Great Clarendon Street
Oxford
OX2 6DP

Dear Sir/Madam,

We are avid fans of your works, particularly the pocket edition of the standard Oxford Dictionary, as we find it helpful, compact and portable.

We have recently been studying the art of pluralisation, using various dictionaries for guidance, and have discovered a few discrepancies which we hope you can clarify for us.

The plural of the word 'cactus':

(**• noun (pl. cacti /kakti/ or cactuses) a succulent plant with a thick fleshy stem bearing spines but no leaves.)** *is, as stated, 'cacti or cactuses.*

Yet, the plural of 'genius':

(**• noun (pl. geniuses) 1 exceptional intellectual or creative power or other natural ability. 2 an exceptionally intelligent or able person),** *in context 1 or 2, is geniuses, as opposed to the expected genii (jee-nee-eye).*

Similarly, the plural of the word penis:

(**• noun (pl. penises or penes /peeneez/) the male organ of copulation and urination.)** *is, as stated 'penes', not peni (peen-eye) as expected.*

We would be extremely appreciative if you could contact us as soon as possible with an explanation for this anomaly in the English language.

We thank you very much for your time, and look forward to hearing from you soon.

Yours in anticipation,

NIKKOLLA JOYYE

KERREINA EVENNS

Academic Division
Managing Director: Tim Barton

Great Clarendon Street
Oxford ox2 6DP
United Kingdom

telephone
fax

www.oup.com

A/Ask Oxford/mc   10 February 2006

Dear Ms Joyye and Ms Evenns,

Thank you for your letter of 8 February to the Oxford Word and Language Service.

Our dictionaries only show the plural form of a word when it is in some way irregular or unusual, so if the plural is not mentioned in the relevant entry it is regular. I am enclosing a photocopy of the section on plural forms in the *Oxford Guide to English Usage* (1992), where the various rules are set out in some detail. The word *genius* has been part of the English language since the Middle English period, and so has a normal plural form.

Usage guides also provide guidance in this area, and I am enclosing copies of the entries for *cactus* and *genius* in the *Pocket Fowler's Modern English Usage* by Robert Allen (OUP 1999). I hope you will find the information helpful.

Yours sincerely,

Margot Charlton (Miss)
Ask Oxford
Oxford English Dictionary

Ms N. Joyye and Ms K. Evenns

Enc.

Oxford University Press is a department of the University of Oxford. It furthers the University's objective of excellence in research, scholarship, and education by publishing worldwide

HARRY BARSTAD
DREW PEACOCK

10 March 2006

British Airways Customer Relations (S506)
PO Box 5619
Sudbury
Suffolk
CO10 2PG

Dear Sir/Madam,

Our very good friends, the gimp and the midget, are planning the trip of a lifetime to Los Angeles in an effort to track down Colin Farrell. Unfortunately, neither of them have flown before (at least not by aeroplane), and they are both petrified.

Please could you forward us some information on relaxation techniques, some reassurance and a list of any appropriate herbal remedies that they can take to combat this paralysing fear?

Thank you very much for you time and information.

Yours,

H BARSTAD

D PEACOCK

BRITISH AIRWAYS

Customer Relations
PO Box 5619 (S506)
Sudbury Suffolk CO10 2PG UK
Tel
Tel
Fax

14 March 2006

Mr Harry Barstad and Mr Drew Peacock

Our Ref: 4549536

Dear Mr Barstad & Mr Peacock

Thank you for writing to us.

We will do our best to make your friends' journey with British Airways as pleasant as possible, but if they do feel nervous at the thought of flying then please check our website - www.britishairways.com for information about what type of help they can find.

I hope your friends will have a pleasant flight with us.

Yours sincerely

Orlette Barneto
Customer Relations

British Airways Plc
Registered Office. Waterside PO Box 365 Harmondsworth UB7 0GB
Registered in England No. 1777777

www.britishairways.com

 member

DREW PEACOCK
HARRY BARSTAD

15 March 2006

Colin Farrell
Creative Artists Agency
9830 Wiltshire Blvd
Beverly Hills CA 90212
USA

Dear Colin

The gimp and the midget have become rather persistent of
late, and have insisted on booking flights to LA to track
you down. The flight is British Airways flight number
BA0279 departing from London Heathrow at 09:55 and
arriving at Los Angeles airport at 12:55 on Monday 08 May
2006.

We courteously suggest that you either meet them at the
airport, preferably dressed in PVC, or you run for your
life, faster than you have ever run before.

Yours,

H BARSTAD

D PEACOCK

And because we're wrong...

NICOLA JOY
KARINA EVANS

28 April 2004

The Really Useful Group
London
WC2H 9TW

Dear Mr Andrew Lloyd Webber and Mr Tim Rice,

It has come to our attention that you have penned a few musicals. We are impressed. Yet, we are unimpressed. Our disappointment stems from the fact that there is a serious lack of musicals about inbreds. We took it upon ourselves to write one. Here is an excerpt (including musical score):

Scene 17

Somewhere in Hillbilly Land, mutant inbreds are lolloping around a camp stove. Some are scratching their huge protruding chins and others are picking their webbed feet. They sing the following song in a Cornish accent:

We are ugly	(la la la laaaaaa)
We are inbreds	(la la la la)
We have webbed feet	(la la laaaaaaaaa la)
And multiple heads	(la laa laalaa laaaaa)
Our chins protrude	(growl growl grrrrrrrr)
Our speech is slurred	(la la lala)
They laugh at us	(la laaaaaaaaaaaaaa la la)
But we are not perturbed	(la la la la laaaaaaaaaaalaaaaaaaaaa)

The inbreds then hug as an act of solidarity, and dance around the camp fire as one.

So far we have had no luck in finding sponsorship for our project. We hope you can help us. We aim to bring awareness to the world about inbreds, their daily struggle to survive even the simplest of tasks, such as shaving their protruding chins, and their amazing talents as goalkeepers/swimmers courtesy of the huge webbed feet. We are planning a National Inbred Awareness Day for next April 1st and hope to have our musical up and running by then.

We look forward to hearing from you soon.

Yours sincerely,

NICOLI JOY
KARINA EVANS

**NICOLA JOY
KARINA EVANS**

12 July 2005

The Really Useful Group
22 Tower Street
London
WC2H 9TW

Dear Mr Andrew Lloyd Webber and Mr Tim Rice,

We sent you a letter some time ago regarding a musical we have penned, yet have heard nothing back from you (Act 17 and original musical score enclosed). We are sorry if you were a little confused; by lolloping we meant dragging their useless limbs behind them. We hope this clears up any confusion for you. We are also a little concerned that perhaps you did not like our original musical score, and so we have amended it to make it a little more pleasing on the ear. The revised musical score, line 2 is now:

la LA la LAAAAAAAAAAAAAAAAAAAAAAAH

instead of the original:

la la la la

Please find below Scene 18 of 'Inbreds- The Musical'

Scene 18

Using the webs on their feet as a springboard, the inbreds launch themselves into the air, squealing with glee, then land in an unfortunate heap on the floor.

Please feel free to not be rude, and reply to this letter.

Yours,

NICOLA JOY

KARINA EVANS

NICOLA JOY
KARINA EVANS

01 November 2005

The Really Useful Group
22 Tower Street
London
WC2H 9TW

Dear Mr Lloyd-Webber and Mr Rice,

We have written to you on two occasions with suggestions and excerpts from our self-penned musical (please find enclosed copies of last two letters), yet have had no reply. The only reason we can think of for this is that you were offended by the layout of our previous letters. This has now been amended, and we are using the 'professional' layout, as opposed to 'modern'. This makes the letter easier on the eye, and, we are sure, almost impossible to not reply to.

As you are no doubt aware, the deadline for our musical has now passed. Luckily, we gave ourselves an extension, and have recently penned the last scene. It is as follows:

SCENE 19

The inbreds are laying in a messy tangle of webbed feet and protruding chins. From stage left skips an angry Eskimo, lower lip hanging in manner of a cod fish. He begins to chant:

DEAD DEAD, INBRED DEAD. DEAD DEAD, INBRED DEAD (Repeat x 30, slowly raising voice to a loud roar whilst pointing at bodies)

Letting out a mighty roar, he rips open his gown to reveal a brief glimpse of micro-member. He then spontaneously combusts.

THE END

We are forever grateful for the feedback that you are undoubtedly about to send us.

Yours,

NICOLA JOY

KARINA EVANS

Dear Tony Blair,

We are not of this world

Hide in your bunker
Hide in your bunker
Hide in your bunker
Hide in your bunker
Hide in your bunker
Hide in your bunker
Hide in your bunker
Hide in your bunker
Hide in your bunker
Hide in your bunker
Hide in your bunker
Hide in your bunker
Hide in your bunker
Hide in your bunker

GAYE SALAMANDER
ROBERTO HANGADOLOFOSTI

21 January 2006

Channel 4 Television
124 Horseferry Road
London
SW1P 2TX

Dear Sir/Madam,

We are writing to you with a fantastic new concept for a reality TV show, which we are confident will be of great interest to you. We are sure that our concept will be successful, as it will appeal to the publics' darker side.

We have filched our idea from a film that we watched recently, which had a unique twist to the reality TV genre. This has inspired us to add a new perspective to the current reality TV craze that is capturing the publics' imagination.

Our contestants will enter a house and live a 'normal' existence in there for up to 8 days. From 8 to 14 days, the contestants will be eliminated one by one until only 5 of the original 14 remain. The contestants will be eliminated by various means, including a secret gas chamber, various poisons and 'accidents'. The surviving contestants will be unaware of the others' demise.

The final five remaining contestants will sit down to a big feast, under the guise of a party. They will then be blown to smithereens by the resident firing squad.

If you feel that this is too immoral for members of the public seeking celebrity, maybe you would feel better about using some 'lifers', and calling the show 'The Inmates'. We are currently seeking permission from the government for the go ahead to use inmates from our nearest prison. We feel snuff is the way forward, and appreciate your views on this matter. Please send correspondence to the above address.

Yours sincerely,

G SALAMANDER

R HANGADOLOFOSTI

Channel 4
124 Horseferry Road
London
SW1P 2TX

Telephone:
Textphone:
channel4.com

Direct Tel:
Direct Fax:

G Salamander & R Hangadolofosti

12 April 2006

VE/MB/PI

Dear Gaye & Roberto,

Thank you for your submission of a new concept for a reality TV show.

We would advise you that Channel 4 do not make the programmes we transmit but commission or purchase them from independent production companies and distributors. Producers are advised to take a look at our producer's website' **www.channel4.co.uk/4producers**

We would suggest that you approach an independent production company with your outline and persuade them to help develop the idea. The television trade newspaper, BROADCAST, publishes a directory called 'The Production Guide' which lists names and addresses of independent production companies. The British Film Institute also publishes a Year Book which lists production companies. PACT (Producer's Alliance for Cinema and Television) publish a handbook with details of their membership which is made up from independent production companies.

Thank you for taking the time and trouble to contact us here at Channel 4, we always welcome interest from our viewers.

Kind regards,

John Burnby
Viewer Enquiries

Channel Four Television Corporation
Luke Johnson, Chairman. Lord Puttnam, Deputy Chairman.
Andy Duncan, Chief Executive. Anne Bulford, Group Finance Director. Andrew Barnes, Sales Director.
Kevin Lygo, Director of Television. Rod Henwood, New Business Director.
Sue Ashtiany, Karren Brady, Tony Hall, Andy Mollett, Martha Lane Fox, Stephen Hill.
Paola Tedaldi, Secretary.

GAYE SALAMANDER
ROBERTO HANGADOLOFOSTI

7 March 2006

Endemol UK
Shepherds Studios-Central
Charecroft Way
Shepherds Bush
London
W14 0EE

Dear Sir/Madam,

We have recently started to watch your programme on Channel 4, entitled Big Brother. Although we are finding it reasonably entertaining, we also feel that it lacks a certain something, and so have devised some cunning plans for you.

We recently watched a film entitled 'My Little Eye', which we thoroughly enjoyed. We recommend it. We have to admit that some of the following ideas were borne from this film, although have been amended slightly to satisfy any copyright criteria.

We have noticed that the punishments doled out by 'Big Brother' do not so much punish as shock. We suggest that contestants are physically punished for any rule breaking that occurs in the 'House'. Our first suggestion is that upon a rule break the contestant is summoned into the 'Diary Room'. The contestant is then shown on a television screen in the main living area, as happened for the nominations last week. The 'Diary Room' is then filled with noxious fumes, preferably green in colour ,and the contestant's slow, agonising death is broadcast live to the housemates. Perhaps there could be a slight time delay as strong contestants may attempt to forcibly enter the 'Diary Room' in order to save their housemate.

Our second and final suggestion is that a contestant is punished for rule breaking by having to pick another 'housemate' to poison. A substance could be slipped into their food or drink and the games begin!

We hope that these ideas are of some help to you, please can you reply by return of post to inform us as to whether you will be using them in this years' series or next.

Yours sincerely,

G SALAMANDER

R HANGADOLOFOSTI

Gaye Salamander
Roberto Hangadolofosti

26 February 2006

Mr Charles Clarke
Home Secretary
Home Office
Direct Communications Unit
2 Marsham Street
London
SW1P 4DF

Dear Mr Clarke,

We are currently developing a reality television show based along the lines of execution. Obviously, we do not want to use ordinary members of the public for this purpose, although we can think of a couple (you know who you are). For this reason, we are asking you for permission to extract 'lifers' to star in this show, thus saving the government lots of money, and entertaining the general public to giant proportions. We feel that this is the way forward, and will certainly rescue our economy.

SAY YES TO SNUFF

We would appreciate your donation and delivery of 'lifers' immediately, and look forward to hearing from you soon.

Thank you for your time.

Yours sincerely,

G SALAMANDER

R HANGADOLOFOSTI

Section
3

...we want new careers and we want

them now

Kat O'Pillaire
Ellie Phante

Random House Group Ltd
20 Vauxhall Bridge Road,
London
SW1V 2SA

10 February 06

Dear Sir/Madam,

We are hoping that you will consider our fantastic manuscript for your kind perusal.

We have written a book on the life of one of the most overlooked insects; the common flea. The book follows 'Flea' from birth and his adventures as he is separated from his family when they all die in fumigation. The book charts his escapades as he is transported all around the globe on various creatures and his narrow escapes from a vengeful fumigator. We are sure you will agree that this is an incredibly unique concept. The book is thrilling, intense and gripping with subtle sentimental undertones.

If you would like to see more, please send correspondence to the above address and we will forward you some chapters. If not, then you must be stark raving bloody mad.

Thank you for your time, we look forward to hearing from you soon

Yours truly,

K O'Pillaire

E Phante

RANDOM HOUSE CHILDREN'S BOOKS

Kat O'Pillaire
Ellie Phante

15th February 2006

Dear Kat,

Thank you for your enquiry about wanting to publish your work with Random House Children's Books.

I'm afraid that at the moment we are only accepting submissions from recognized literary agents. A list can be found in the *Children's Writers' and Artists' Yearbook*, which is available in libraries and bookshops and contains a lot of useful information for first-time authors.

Sorry to disappoint you on this matter, but we wish you luck in placing your work elsewhere.

Yours sincerely,

Editorial Department
<u>Random House Children's Books</u>

JONATHAN CAPE

HUTCHINSON

BODLEY HEAD

DOUBLEDAY

DAVID FICKLING BOOKS

CORGI

RED FOX

61 - 63 Uxbridge Road
London W5 5SA
Tel:
Fax:

Website: www.kidsatrandomhouse.co.uk

Registered No: 954009
Registered Office
20 Vauxhall Bridge Road, London SW1V 2SA

A DIVISION OF THE RANDOM HOUSE GROUP LTD

Kat O'Pillaire
Ellie Phante

Random House Group Ltd
20 Vauxhall Bridge Road
London
SW1V 2SA

19th February 2006

Dear Sir/Madam

We recently wrote to you regarding our unique concept on our book about the
adventures of 'Flea'. We have just received a rejection from your children's book
department. We think you have greatly misunderstood us; our book is intended for
mature adults of sane minds and can be marketed as fiction. As we stated in our
previous letter (copy enclosed), our book is thrilling, intense and gripping and you
would be mad not to accept it. Please forward our letters to the appropriate
department.

Thank you for your time, we look forward to hearing positive news from you soon.

Yours truly

Kat O'Pilliare

Ellie Phante

Karina Evans & Nicola Joy

06/02/06

Tony Blair
10 Downing Street
London

Dear Mr Blair,

We know that you are a very busy man but we are hoping that you would
be kind enough to take the time to give us some guidance. We would one
day like to be Prime Minister as we know we would do a great job at
shaping up the country. Can you please tell us how we would go about
this, as we know nothing about politics and just want to rule the world.

Thank you for your time, we look forward to hearing from you soon,

Yours seriously

Karina Evans

Nicola Joy

PS. Do aliens exist? We are sure we saw one in our back garden last
Tuesday, it was precisely 19.41, we could send you an artist's impression
if this is any help.

10 DOWNING STREET
LONDON SW1A 2AA

From the Direct Communications Unit

20 March 2006

Karina Evans

Dear Karina

The Prime Minister has asked me to thank you and Nicola for your recent letter.

Mr Blair would like to reply personally, but as you will appreciate he receives many thousands of letters each week and this is not possible.

On the issue of becoming an MP, first you must decide which political party you wish to represent, you could then join a local youth group for that party. Details of theses groups should be available at your local library. You can then progress through the group and when you are old enough, stand for selection as a candidate to represent the party of your choice. Additionally, so you may like to look at the Youth Parliament website: www.ukyouthparliament.org.uk which is aimed at young people aged between 11 and 18 and has a wealth of information you may find useful.

Yours sincerely

F Jones

F JONES

Karina Evans & Nicola Joy

20 April 2006

Tony Blair
Direct Communications Unit
10 Downing Street
London
SW1A 2AA

Dear F

We recently wrote to Tony Blair asking how to become Prime Minister. Upon reading your reply we were utterly shocked and humiliated that you assumed us to be of under average adult intelligence and classified us in the age range of 11-18 yrs. We are in fact almost thirty. We are also astounded that you blatantly ignored our inquiry regarding the existence of aliens.

We have enclosed a copy of the original letter we sent you and correspondence. We would be very grateful if you could send us another reply, this time taking our true ages into consideration.

Thank you for your time, we look forward to receiving our new reply soon.

Yours

Karina Evans

Nicola Joy

1O DOWNING STREET
LONDON SW1A 2AA

From the Direct Communications Unit   10 May 2006

Karina Evans

Dear Ms Evans

I am writing to thank you and Ms Joy for your letter of 20 April. I am sorry that our previous reply of 20 March assumed that you were of a younger age.

Regarding your question on how to become Prime Minister, you will first need to join and become actively involved within a political party of your choice. Information about political parties can be found at your local library or on the internet. Most political parties offer the opportunity to stand for selection as a local councillor. Becoming a councillor will enable you to gain some political experience and useful skills in public speaking, debating and problem solving. Your political party will be also be able to advise you on other opportunities in order to further your political career.

Your comments about aliens have been noted. The Ministry of Defence is responsible for this subject and you may wish to visit their website for more information: http://www.mod.uk

Yours sincerely

M Davies

M DAVIES

Karina Evans & Nicola Joy

18/05/06

M.O.D Ministerial Correspondence Unit
5th Floor, Zone A
Main Building
Whitehall
London
SW1A 2HB

Dear Sir/Madam

We recently wrote to the Prime Minister after we thought we saw an alien outside our kitchen window. It was one Tuesday at precisely 7.41pm. He could not help us and advised we write to you, we were wondering if you could please tell us do aliens really exist or did we both imagine the same thing? This incident has left us quivering and disturbed.

Thank you for your time, we look forward to your immediate response.

Yours truly,

Karina Evans

Nicola Joy

P.S. We can forward an artist's impression if this is of any help.

From: Mrs J Monk
Directorate of Air Staff – Freedom of Information 1

MINISTRY OF DEFENCE
5th Floor, Zone H, Main Building, Whitehall, London SW1A 2HB

Telephone	(Direct dial)
	(Switchboard)
	(Fax)

Ms Karina Evans & Ms Nicola Joy

Your Reference:

Our Reference:
D/DAS/64/2
Date:
05 June 2006

Dear Ms Evans & Ms Joy

I am writing with reference to your report of alien phenomena seen on 16 May 2006, the details of which you passed to the Ministerial Correspondence Unit. This office is the focal point within the Ministry of Defence for correspondence relating to 'UFOs.'

First, it may be helpful if I explain that the Ministry of Defence examines any reports of 'unidentified flying objects' it receives solely to establish whether what was seen might have some defence significance; namely, whether there is any evidence that the United Kingdom's airspace might have been compromised by hostile or unauthorised air activity.

Unless there is evidence of a potential threat to the United Kingdom from an external source, and to date no 'UFO' report has revealed such evidence, we do not attempt to identify the precise nature of each sighting reported to us. We believe that rational explanations, such as aircraft lights or natural phenomena, could be found for them if resources were diverted for this purpose, but it is not the function of the MOD to provide this kind of aerial identification service. It would be an inappropriate use of defence resources if we were to do so.

The MOD does not have any expertise or role in respect of 'UFO/flying saucer' matters to the question of the existence or otherwise of extraterrestrial life forms, about which it remains totally open-minded. I should add that to date, the MOD knows of no evidence which substantiates the existence of these alleged phenomena.

With regard to your particular observation, I can confirm that we received no other reports of this alien phenomena from anywhere in the UK.

Sorry I could not be any help.

Yours sincerely

J. Monk.

Gordon and Henrietta Bear-Bottom

The British Board of Film Classification
3 Soho Square
London W1D 3HD

08 February 2006

Dear Sir/Madam,

We are both in our twenties and have recently been going through what some
would describe as quarter life crises. We have challenged everything that we hold
dear, and dumped everything that no longer fulfils us, including our jobs. We have
been searching for the perfect career for some time now. Last Thursday at exactly
twelve noon we drew a conclusion; we both enjoy watching films and eating
popcorn, so therefore the perfect career for us would be film classifiers.

Ideally, we would like to work from home, for large sums of money. If you could
forward us some films, a cheque and classification guidelines by return of post it
would be much appreciated.

We enjoy all types of film but are particularly eager to classify the ones starring
Colin Farrell.

We look forward to hearing from you soon,

Yours with anticipation,

G Bear-Bottom

H Bear-Bottom

British Board of Film Classification 3 Soho Square London W1D 3HD t: f: http://www.bbfc.co.uk

09 March 2006

Mr & Mrs Bear-Bottom

Dear Sir and Madam,

Thank you for your letter dated 08 February and I apologise for the late response.

All BBFC vacancies are advertised on our dedicated website –
http://www.londonjobvacancies.co.uk – and it is worthwhile checking the site periodically.

There are no Examiner vacancies at present, although we do have two vacancies, Personnel Office Manager and Information Systems Specialist. If you are interested, all the information can be found on the website.

I hope you find this information useful and we thank you for your interest in our work.

Yours sincerely,

Jennifer Robotham
Administrative Officer (Personnel)

Karina Evans & Nicola Joy

Philips Electronics U.K. Ltd   02/11/05
Guildford
Surrey
GU2 8XH

Dear Sir/Madam

We are writing in hope that you will kindly consider our proposal for a pioneering new invention. The Eggsmaid.

Our invention will change the way people wake in the morning. Instead of waking to an annoying alarm clock they can wake to an annoying alarm clock and a cooked breakfast. We believe a hot breakfast is a very good incentive for one to rise, especially on a cold winter morning. The Eggsmaid is an alarm clock complete with a heating surface on top. Before you go to sleep at night you crack open an egg or two and place it/them on top of the Eggsmaid, there is also some room for some raw bacon. Ten minutes before the alarm is due to go off the Eggsmaid starts to get hot, very hot, cooking the eggs and bacon. We haven't worked out how this will work yet, we are hoping that your electronics experts will be able to assist us in this matter. We have had a few thoughts though, perhaps some sort of short circuiting device on a timer that will start to overheat. We feel that the Eggsmaid will revolutionise the way we eat breakfast; it is a modern day version of the age old trick of cooking eggs on your car engine. This will negate the need of shuffling to your car in a dressing gown in the wee hours.

We are also working on an idea for the Summersmaid, this is a similar concept to the Eggsmaid, but instead of a hot surface it has a blender on its head that you place fruit in before you go to bed. You can then wake up to a delicious fruit smoothie. A very healthy start to the day, we are sure you'll agree.

We are approaching Philips first because of its excellent reputation; we hope that you will agree to collaborate with us on this venture. If you like we can forward you some basic diagrams, maybe we can then arrange an exploratory meeting. In the unlikely event that you do not wish to explore this idea further we would appreciate it if you would let us know as soon as possible. We can then approach other companies with this fabulous new idea. We would also be very grateful for any feedback on our ideas or any other information you think would be beneficial to us. Thank you for your time.

We look forward to hearing from you soon.

Karina Evans & Nicola Joy

PHILIPS

Philips Electronics UK Limited

Philips Centre, Guildford Business Park, Guildford, Surrey GU2 8XH

Karina Evans & Nicola Joy

Chairman's Office
Tel:
Fax:

Ref:
Date: 30th November 2005

Dear Ms' Evans & Joy

Thank you for your letter dated 2nd November 2005.

Although it is unlikely that we would consider taking this issue any further, I am forwarding your letter on to our Domestic Appliances division for their consideration.

If they have an interest in your ideas then they will contact you directly.

Yours sincerely

Gail Sandifer
PA to The Chairman
For and on behalf of
Philips Electronics UK Ltd

Philips Electronics UK Limited
Registered in England No. 446897
Registered office
Philips Centre, Guildford Business Park
Guildford, Surrey GU2 8XH
www.philips.com

INVESTOR IN PEOPLE

PHILIPS

Philips Intellectual Property & Standards

Cross Oak Lane, Redhill, Surrey RH1 5HA, United Kingdom.

Karina Evans & Nichola Joy

Tel:
Fax:

Ref. AGW/KM
Date: 2005.12.16

Dear Ms' Evans & Joy,

Your letter dated 2nd November 2005 addressed to Philips Electronics UK Ltd., Guildford has been passed to this Department which handles the initial evaluation of all unsolicited proposals for product innovation received in the UK from outside the Company.

Firstly we would like to thank you for considering Philips in relation to your idea. As a Company we are very committed to continuous innovation in and improvement of our products and we are also interested to hear from members of the public who have ideas for product innovation which may be of interest to us.

As you will no doubt appreciate we receive many approaches from persons outside the Company offering us ideas for possible commercial exploitation. In order to safeguard the interests of private inventors as well as those of the Company, we have found it necessary to make it a rule to consider only those ideas which have been protected by the filing of a patent application at the UK Patent Office.

If you decide to seek patent protection we will then be willing to consider your ideas. In that case we would ask you to send the specification of your patent application, i.e. the description and the drawings you filed with your application, and, at least initially, no other information about your ideas. However, we wish to make it clear that it is entirely a matter for you to decide whether or not to apply for patent protection and that we can assume no responsibility for any costs you may incur.

We enclose two brochures issued by the UK Patent Office ("Patents Essential Reading" and "Patents Application Guide") which you might find useful, should you decide to seek patent protection for your ideas.

The Company will accept the submission of your specification only on the basis that if the Company decides not to come to an arrangement with you no claim whatsoever will be made against the Company (or any of its subsidiary or associated companies) in respect of an invention other than in an action for infringement of a patent resulting from a patent application covering the invention.

Philips Electronics UK Limited
Registered in England No. 446897
Registered office
Philips Centre, Guildford Business Park
Guildford, Surrey GU2 8XH
www.philips.com

PHILIPS

Page 2

If your idea is of interest, then of course we would agree with you the conditions on which further discussions may take place.

We cannot accept any submission as a disclosure in confidence, particularly since we may already be working on a similar idea in one of our research or development programmes. Nonetheless, we will take all reasonable precautions to prevent unauthorised disclosure of your submission. We would point out that it is sometimes necessary for us to send your specification to our parent company in The Netherlands for consideration.

Finally, please forgive us for making this such a complicated matter. We certainly do not wish to obtain new and useful information for nothing, but much information is thought by inventors to be new, when it is in fact known to the public or to us or is obvious in the light of what is known. We are of course free to use such types of information. We believe that the conditions set out in this letter are fair and reasonable in order to protect both you and ourselves and fairly cover the possible circumstances.

I look forward to hearing further from you.

Yours sincerely,

Kndle

for A. G. White

Enc.

Karina Evans & Nicola Joy

A.G. White
Philips Intellectual property and standards
Cross Oak Lane,
Redhill
Surrey
RH1 5HA

06/01/06

Dear A.G. White

Thank you for your useful, yet confusing letter dated 2005.12.16 and accompanying brochures providing information on patenting our idea, the Eggsmaid. We have read the literature but have encountered a few problems. Firstly we discovered that we would need to submit some diagrams; neither of us can draw. Nor can we afford to pay an illustrator; in fact we don't even know one. Secondly, we have no idea of how the Eggsmaid would actually work, neither of us have any sort of background in circuitry or electrics. This is why we are contacting you again, in hope that there is a loophole somewhere that we could exploit? For example, we could team up with your company boffins and designed the Eggsmaid together then patent it as a joint venture? That way everybody will be kept happy; Philips will be recognised to be the very best when it comes the most innovative cutting edge gadgets and we will be plump of pocket. It's a win win situation; everyone gets to benefit. We do hope that you will consider this proposal. By the way Nicola is spelt without an h.

Thank you for your time. We look forward to hearing from you soon.

Yours with anticipation

Karina Evans

Nicola Joy

PHILIPS

Philips Intellectual Property & Standards

Cross Oak Lane, Redhill. Surrey RH1 5HA. United Kingdom.

Ms. K. Evans & Ms. N. Joy

Tel:
Fax:

Ref: AGW/KM
Date: 2006-01-16

Dear Ms Evans & Ms. Joy,

Thank you for your further letter of 6th January 2006 regarding your idea for an "Eggsmaid".

We regret to inform you that we are not interested in taking your idea any further as we have some concerns regarding the health and safety risks of locating a hotplate next to a sleeping person and the hygiene aspects associated with uncovered raw food held at room temperature overnight.

However, we thought you may be interested to know that the idea of egg frying devices has already been invented as described in the enclosed patent specifications which show a variety of devices for cooking eggs, one dating back as far as 1930.

Thank you, again, for giving us the opportunity to consider your idea.

Yours sincerely,

Kndler

for A. G. White

Enc: US Patent 1,986,412
US Patent 2,517,167
US Patent 3,541,947
US Patent 2,670,674
US Patent 1,120,749

Philips Electronics UK Limited
Registered in England No. 446897
Registered office
Philips Centre, Guildford Business Park
Guildford, Surrey GU2 8XH
www.philips.com

Karina Evans & Nicola Joy

A.G.White
Philips Intellectual Property & Standards
Cross Oak Lane,
Redhill,
Surrey
RH1 5HA

Ref: AGW/KM
27/01/06

Dear A.G.White

Thank you for your letter dated 16/01/06. We are concerned that you think our Eggsmaid is dangerous and unhygienic. We are also dismayed that we will have to go back to frying eggs on our car engine. But nonetheless as we are avid inventors and never the type to give up at the first hurdle, we are back with a new proposition for a new invention. We would like to present to you the Cerealmaid, the reasoning behind it is the same as the Eggsmaid. Breakfast will be prepared for the consumer on waking. The consumer will program the Cerealmaid with the alarm time and load it with cereal the night before, thus saving them the tedious task of walking to the kitchen to get their breakfast the next morning. In place of the hot plate will be a chilled compartment and a mechanical arm that will pour the milk on the cereal when the consumer wakes. We do hope that this safer invention will be more suited to your company and hope that you and the boffins at Philips will consider taking this idea further. We are sure you will appreciate that with our active minds, we will not stop inventing until we have revolutionised breakfast time. Any feedback on our latest concept will be most appreciated.

Thank you for your time. We look forward to hearing from you soon.

Yours sincerely

Karina Evans

Nicola Joy

NICOLA & KARINA

15 April 2006

HarperCollins Publishers Ltd
77-85 Fulham Palace Road
London
W6 8JB

Dear Poetry Publisher,

We are writing to you in the hope that you can help us fulfil our dream. We have just realised that we are rather talented poetry writers. We are trying to be noticeable in the world of amateur poetry by writing something other than a limerick or Haiku.

We have amazed ourselves with the following poem. This work of art started out as a song, but unfortunately does not fit properly to 'London's Burning'; the only tune we can play on the keyboard.

Grandma

Every time I see you
I get scared
Your face is so minging
Wrinkly and scarred

Grandma, you're old
But still alive
You looked so normal
When I was five

Grandma, it's time to go
Time to leave this mortal coil
You're weird and you scare me
With your grey lips, and Olay oil

Grandma, Grandma
Grandma, Grandma
You're weird, yes you are
Grandma, Grandma
Grandma, Grandma   *(to fade)*

This is obviously a small, yet excellent, sample of our work. We will forward you 'Pebbles', 'Black Cat in A Teapot', and 'The Man With The Iron Fingernails' as soon as we have them typed up. They are currently written in jam on the kitchen wall.

Regardless of whether you are happy to publish our poetry, we would appreciate some constructive feedback. We are still amateurs, and although talented, would deeply appreciate some guidance.

Thank you very much for your time,

We look forward to hearing from you soon,

NICOLA

KARINA

HarperCollins

77-85 FULHAM PALACE ROAD.
HAMMERSMITH LONDON W6 8JB
T
F
www.harpercollins.co.uk

3/5/06

Dear ~~Sir/Madam~~, Nicole & Karine

Thank you for your letter and for giving us the opportunity to consider your work.

We write to inform you that, regrettably, we very rarely publish a poetry book, but the **WRITERS' AND ARTISTS' YEARBOOK** (published by A & C Black) will give you the names of those publishers who do. However, our understanding is that even they tend not to publish books by 'new' writers. What you may need to do, and again the Yearbook should help you here, is first to submit individual poems to journals and magazines and then, perhaps, move into the book market.

We hope the above information will be helpful to you and wish you best of luck in placing your work.

Yours faithfully,

pp. **HARPER COLLINS PUBLISHERS**

REGISTERED AS HARPERCOLLINS PUBLISHERS LTD (SCOTLAND 1949 NO. 27388). WESTERHILL ROAD, BISHOPBRIGGS, GLASGOW G64 2QT

| HARPERCOLLINS | HARPER PERENNIAL | COLLINS WILLOW | VOYAGER | THORSONS | COLLINS |
| FOURTH ESTATE | HARPERCOLLINS ENTERTAINMENT | HARPERCOLLINS AUDIO | HARPERCOLLINS CHILDREN'S BOOKS | ELEMENT | TIMES BOOKS |

'SHARKY' AND 'WILLY'

24 February 2006

WARNER CHAPPELL MUSIC GROUP LTD
161 Hammersmith Road
London

Dear Sir/Madam,

We are approaching you with regards to a song that we have written, which we feel is good enough to be sung by a top artist. For this reason we are submitting it to you for feedback and forwarding to the appropriate artist. We know that showbiz is a scary world and so we shall henceforth be known solely by our first names. These have, in turn, been changed to protect us.

Although we are obviously extraordinarily talented, we cannot write music. We have no musical instruments of our own, bar a glockenspiel. We have discovered that the following song fits perfectly to the tune of the Bee Gee's classic 'How Deep Is Your Love'. Alternatively, if you would like us to write songs with original music we would appreciate it if you forwarded us a list of musical composers along with our feedback.

How Big Is My Bum?

When I wake up in the morning sun
I go and cook my eggs in the frying pan
And the moment that the smoke alarm goes off
I know I wanna stuff my face again
I come to you, eggs all over my face
And I keep the toast warm in my special place
And it's now I need to say
How big is my bum?
Is my bum
How big is my bum?
I really need to know
'Cos I've told you that I'm a size eight
You know the truth
I am a size twenty two
I have been lying to you

Thank you very much for your time, we look forward to hearing from you soon.

'SHARKY' & 'WILLY'

GAYE SALAMANDER
ROBERTO HANGADOLOFOSTI

16 February 2006

Big Little Poem Books
3 Park Avenue
Melton Mowbray
Leics
LE13 0JB

Dear Fellow poet,

We are currently reviewing the path that we wish to follow in life, and after much thought, tears and many arguments, we have decided that poetry is the path to take. For this reason, and this reason alone, we have penned some poetry for your scrutiny.

Man Called Paul

There was once a man called Paul
Precariously perched on a wall
He had a heart attack
Which took him aback
And he suffered a fatal fall

Girl Called Skye

There was once a girl called Skye
Who looked a bit like a fly
People pointed and stared
Which rendered her scared
So she had a bit of a cry

Man Called Sharky

There was a short man called 'Sharky'
Who decided to have a party
His guests all got pissed
Got raunchy and kissed
He said, 'I'm not digging this malarkey'

Drink Called Wine

There is a drink called wine
Which is incredibly fine
But if you drink it too quickly
It gets a bit sickly
And you sometimes forget the time

We understand that you may be a little dissatisfied as the poems are all limericks. To showcase our talent, and to demonstrate our versatility, we have penned the following poem. It is not a limerick. It is a haiku.

Washing Day

Washing in machine
Whirring round and round and round
Launder dirt away

We are understandably delighted with our attempts at poetry and would like to have our work published. For this reason we are submitting the above poems to you for perusal, feedback and publishing.

We look forward to hearing from you soon.

Yours in anticipation,

G Salamander

G SALAMANDER

R HANGADOLOFOSTI

The Big Little Poem Series

Editor: Robert Richardson

Thank you for submitting your work. Unfortunately the list is "full up" for the next few years.

good luck elsewhere

ROSITA ROSE
PRITI PANZIE

14 February 2006

Bad Press
43 Kingsdown House
Amhurst Road
London
E8 2AS

Dear Friend,

We are both aspiring poets, but are finding it incredibly difficult to break into the beautiful world of poetry. We have written hundreds of poems over the last few hours, and are submitting two of our best, 'Heading South' and 'Pebbles' to you with a view to having them published. We are confident that you will be interested in them, although if you are not we would appreciate some feedback.

HEADING SOUTH

Sitting on my doorstep
A lonely face
Smoking a fag
A lonely place
Starting to sag
My beautiful face
Cat's arse mouth
Heading south
Everywhere
Heading south
Heading south
My beautiful body
Heading south
Time for another drag
Where's my bag?
Smoke a fag
Another drag
Another fag
Sag
Sag
Sag

PEBBLES

Pebbles on the beach
Pebbles on the beach
Waves crashing
A lonely leech
Pebbles on the beach

We appreciate your time, and wait in eagerness for your reply,

Yours,

R ROSE

P PANZIE

Nicola Joy & Karina Evans

Mohammed Al Fayed
Harrods
Knightsbridge
London

06 Dec. 05

Dear Mr Al Fayed

We are writing in hope that you will be able to assist us on our journey into the fashion world.

We have always dreamt of dressing the world. Our ambition is to make everybody look as good as we do. We feel that maybe you could be the spring board to our success. We have some fabulous and innovative ideas for designs for the forthcoming season, here are just two of them; vibrating furry deck shoes that come in an assortment of bright funky colours, and a shirt with a detachable hairy chest wig that also doubles as a toupee/ hairy hat in different strengths of hairiness for the follically challenged. What could be better then having a foot massage every time you put your shoes on or having a spare bouffant to whip out every time your head gets cold? We are sure you'll agree, these are fabulous ideas. We do not have a background in fashion as such, but we do have a keen eye for style and are way ahead of the times. You can see this by the aforementioned ideas. We feel our creative flair and vast imaginations can only be a huge asset to your company, and if we do not break into the fashion world we feel our talents will have been cruelly wasted. In the highly unlikely event that you do not wish to explore our ideas further please would you let us know as soon as possible so that we can approach other companies. We have enclosed a sae for your speedy reply.

Thank you for your time, we look forward to working with you soon.

Yours truly

Nicola Joy

Karina Evans

Nicola Joy & Karina Evans

20th December 2005

Dear Ms Joy & Ms Evans

I write in response to your letter dated 6th December 2005, which was addressed to the Chairman, Mr Al Fayed.

I would like to thank you for the introduction to your business and the details of the brand which were passed on to the Womenswear department.

We are currently reviewing our brand selection, but feel that at present your product mix does not fit in with our current plans. Should this change in the future, we will contact you.

We would like to wish you all the very best for the future and would like to thank you for your interest in Harrods.

Yours sincerely

PP Allen.

Marigay McKee
Director – Fashion & Beauty
Harrods Ltd

Nicola Joy & Karina Evans

Mr Al Fayed
Harrods Limited
Knightsbridge
London
SW1X 7XL

08/01/06

Dear Sir

We recently sent a letter addressed personally to you, Mr Al Fayed, regarding our truly outstanding fashion concepts. Obviously from the correspondence we received back from your store you did not get to read it for yourself. We were shocked when we received notification from your store dated 20th December 2005 informing us that our 'brand' had been passed on to the womenswear department...? We hate to think what type of woman frequents your store if that's where you think our shirts with detachable hairy chest wigs belong. We do not think your staff have taken our proposal very seriously at all, or even read our original letter properly; our ideas are quite obviously aimed at men. We have enclosed a copy of the original letter and reply for you to peruse. We are disturbed and perturbed, if one of the biggest stores in the world won't take us seriously, who will?

We are very hurt and would like a very full explanation. Thank you for your time.

Yours with rejected sour faces, sadness, sorrow, forlornness, misery, rage and rue

Nicola Joy

Karina Evans

Karina Evans & Nicola Joy

Now
IPC Media
Stamford Street
London
SE1 9LS

26 November 2005

Dear Sir/Madam

We are at pivotal points in our careers and full of lustful thoughts. We thought that it would be a wise idea to combine these two factors and start working for you. We come as a team as we work at our best together. We are inquisitive by nature and our punctuation is second to none as is our wit. For these reasons we feel that we would be ideal for a position as a celebrity interviewer. Although we would refuse to interview ugly orange celebrities with perma-tans, we would be more than willing to interview the likes of Colin Farrell naked.

We are available for an immediate start, and can provide excellent references from our time spent in the army under the ever watchful eye of Lieutenant Stampard of the Royal Military Corp. We refuse to work for no less than 45K per annum and expect first class travel and a finger buffet to be provided when we have to go to L.A. to interview Hollywood stars. We are sure you will agree that we are exceptionally talented and therefore do not need to go through the rigmarole of the application/interview process. In the most unlikely event that you do not want to employ us we would appreciate it if you could let us know immediately so that we can start approaching other magazines that interview celebrities. We have enclosed a sae for your speedy reply.

Thank you for your time, we look forward to joining your company soon.

Yours with anticipation

Karina Evans

Nicola Joy

5th December 2005

Karina Evans and Nicola Joy

Dear Karina and Nicola,

Thank you for writing to us regarding work opportunities with *Now*.

Unfortunately we do not have any positions which would be suitable for you at present, but we will keep your letter on file and contact you should that change.

With best wishes,

Yours sincerely

Laura Pollard
Magazine Assistant

IPC Connect Limited, King's Reach Tower, Stamford Street, London SE1 9LS
Switchboard: Web site: http://www.ipcmedia.com

A part of IPC Media, a Time Warner company

Registered Office as above. Registered Number: 3784704 England.

**PETRA LESIONS
CINDY CORTEX**

02 March 2006

Paul Lamond Toys and Games Ltd
3 Newington Green
London
N16 9PU

To whom it may concern,

We are writing to you regarding a board game we have designed which we are sure you will be interested in. We have briefly outlined it below, and are hoping to arrange a meeting with yourselves with a view to marketing it.

THE BRAIN

The board consists of a 39 brightly coloured squares, two boxes in which to put 'Ouch' and 'Get off my land' cards, and in the centre of the board sits a huge pulsating brain. We have discussed the material that we feel suitable for the brain, and have come to the conclusion that in order to obtain the authentic wobbling/pulsating, the brain should be made out of jelly. This, of course, shall be covered in a protective cling film, thus ensuring that no young children consume it. If this is too technical then we suggest that perhaps the British Medical Institute may have authentic pickled brains that they no longer have use for.

AIM OF THE GAME

The aim of the game is to advance around the board without disturbing 'Brain', using a variety of dice throws, action squares and aforementioned 'Ouch' and 'Get off my land' cards. If the player gets too close to the brain, and the brain realises, it will become offended. When offended, 'Brain' expands to 27 times its normal size, a big red siren (similar to those used on American police vehicles) ascends out of the cortex area and a 1000 decibel screech emanates from the frontal lobe (for this reason we feel it would be advisable to include ear protection in the box). There is then is a lull whilst 'Brain' reverts back to his usual size. It then whispers, in a Cornish accent, 'Get off my land, I'll swing for you, I will', and game play resumes.

We are sure you will agree that this is a fantastic idea, and we look forward to hearing from you soon with suggestions on how to proceed with this proposal.

Yours faithfully,

Petra Lesions

PETRA LESIONS

Cortex

CINDY CORTEX

GAYE SHORT-PERRSON
PARIS PARRIS

MB Games
Hasbro UK Ltd
Caswell Way
Newport
Gwent
NP19 4YH

10 January 2006

Dear Sir/Madam,

We are writing to you with a proposal for a board game which we feel you will be interested in. We have noticed that in recent years there has been a surge in the cosmetic surgery industry, and that a lot of people now want to work in this field. We have a unique proposal for a board game which would interest this large corner of the market.

THE GAME

The game is to be called 'Plastic Surgeon', and is for 2 - 4 adult players. It is played using a variety of dice throws, action cards and 'surgery squares'.

AIM OF THE GAME

The aim of the game is to successfully operate on the protruding, regenerative, rubber face that is in the middle of the board, proceed through the ranks to become 'Extra Super Surgeon', and earn the gilt coat. The type of surgery is based on which 'surgery square' you land on, or which action card you pick up. The types of surgery vary from a simple eyebrow lift, to a more complex full face lift. As mentioned previously, the protruding, rubber face has regenerative qualities, and so real surgical instruments, such as scalpels, can be used. For this reason, we recommend that the game be marketed at the over 18s, or to only be used under adult supervision. Scalpels are very sharp.

If the player completes the surgery correctly, in the allotted time (stated on the action card or 'surgery square'), then the rubber face squeals in delight, and the player advances along the board and gets a 'Super Surgeon' coat to put on his playing piece. If the surgery is conducted incorrectly, or the time runs out, then the face sadly sings 'I ain't got no body, no, no, no, I ain't got no body, no, no, no, my face is mutated, woe, woe, woe', the player moves back several squares, and any 'Super Surgeon' coats previously earned are returned.

If a player unsuccessfully operates 3 times in a row, then he is sacked and has to play one round in the capacity of hospital cleaner. This involves picking up bits of rubber and putting them back onto the face in order for it to start the regenerative process.

We are very excited at the prospect of this game, and are certain that you are the people to manufacture it. Please can you reply as soon as possible, as in the unlikely event that you do not wish to take this proposal further, we will approach other manufacturers.

Thank you for you time, we look forward to hearing from you soon.

Yours in anticipation,

GAYE SHORT-PERRSON

PARIS PARRIS

CONSUMER AFFAIRS
HASBRO UK LTD.
P.O. BOX 43
NEWPORT
NP19 4YD
FREEPHONE
TEL:
FAX:
www.hasbro.co.uk

REF 0275316A

January 16, 2006

Mr Perrson

Dear Mr Perrson,

We are in receipt of your recent letter, which has been passed to us for reply. Hasbro thank you for inviting them to consider your idea, however, the company maintains a very strict policy against reviewing such unsolicited proposals from individual inventors.

We suggest you contact a toy and games agent who represents the concepts and prototypes of independent inventors to various manufacturers throughout the toy and games industry or **The British Toy and Hobby Association** in the UK. Outside of the UK, a local Trade Association may be able to provide a list of agents for you who may sell the proposed new product within the industry.

The British Toy and Hobby Association however, produce an "<u>Inventor Pack</u>", which contains a comprehensive listing of members and allied service companies. They also produce a further book entitled <u>The Toy Industry in the United Kingdom</u>, which contains a section especially for games inventors. For further information on availability and pricing you may wish to contact them at **80 Camberwell Road, London, SE5 OEG, Tel:** ⬛⬛⬛⬛⬛ . In the meantime we cannot make a specific recommendation and do not endorse any of the agents mentioned, we are attaching a list of names and addresses of agents who have given us permission to release their names.

CONSUMER AFFAIRS
HASBRO UK LTD.
P.O. BOX 43
NEWPORT
NP19 4YD
FREEPHONE
TEL:
FAX:
www.hasbro.co.uk

0275316A
Page 2

We are returning any materials and correspondence you sent us, which we can confirm have neither been copied, examined nor reviewed. We wish you well with your efforts to market your concept.

Yours Sincerely

Consumer Affairs Advisor
Hasbro Consumer Affairs

GAYE SHORT-PERRSON
PARIS PARRIS

8 February 2006

MB Games
Hasbro UK Ltd
Caswell Way
Newport
Gwent
NP19 4YH

Dear Sir /Madam,

We write to you regarding a proposal we sent you recently for a game entitled
'Plastic Surgeon' (proposal enclosed). Shortly after sending you this proposal, we
received a standard, non-offensive rejection letter.

We are writing to you as we are a little confused. We feel that our game is innovative
, unique and undoubtedly worthy of manufacture. For this reason, your standard
rejection letter cunningly disguised as a list of games agents has upset us.

We have realised that it is not the quality of the game that is the problem, it is either
the cost of manufacturing such an advanced product, or problems making the
protruding, regenerative face. We are currently in the process of submitting our
proposal to other companies, and are concerned that if the game is not feasible
then we are wasting our time.

Please could you contact us as soon as possible to let us know for which reason ,
other than us not possessing an agent, you will not consider manufacturing our
product.

We look forward to hearing from you soon.

Yours faithfully,

G SHORT-PERRSON

P PARRIS

CONSUMER AFFAIRS
HASBRO UK LTD.
P.O. BOX 43
NEWPORT
NP19 4YD
FREEPHONE
TEL:
FAX:
www.hasbro.co.uk

REF 02753168

February 14, 2006

Mr Perrson

Dear Mr Perrson,

We are in receipt of your recent letter, which has been passed to us for reply. Hasbro thank you for inviting them to consider your idea, however, the company maintains a very strict policy against reviewing such unsolicited proposals from individual inventors.

We suggest you contact a toy and games agent who represents the concepts and prototypes of independent inventors to various manufacturers throughout the toy and games industry or **The British Toy and Hobby Association** in the UK. Outside of the UK, a local Trade Association may be able to provide a list of agents for you who may sell the proposed new product within the industry.

The British Toy and Hobby Association however, produce an "<u>Inventor Pack</u>", which contains a comprehensive listing of members and allied service companies. They also produce a further book entitled <u>The Toy Industry in the United Kingdom</u>, which contains a section especially for games inventors. For further information on availability and pricing you may wish to contact them at **80 Camberwell Road, London, SE5 0EG, Tel:** . In the meantime we cannot make a specific recommendation and do not endorse any of the agents mentioned, we are attaching a list of names and addresses of agents who have given us permission to release their names.

GAYE SHORT-PERRSON
PARIS PARRIS

MB Games
Hasbro UK Ltd
Caswell Way
Newport
Gwent
NP19 4YH

7 March 2006

Dear Sir/Madam,

We have had occasion to write to you a couple of times recently, and have made an unfortunate discovery that shocks us to the core. On both occasions that we corresponded with you, you sent us the very same reply. Is there something wrong with your computer/secretary? Or is it sheer complacency on your part? We think that now is the time to buck your ideas up and be imaginative.

We look forward to our personalised reply.

Yours truly,

G SHORT-PERRSON

P PARRIS

CONSUMER AFFAIRS
HASBRO UK LTD.
P.O. BOX 43
NEWPORT
NP19 4YD
FREEPHONE
TEL:
FAX:
www.hasbro.co.uk

REF 0275316C

March 22, 2006

Mr Perrson

Dear Mr Perrson,

Thank you for your recent letter to Hasbro UK Ltd regarding our previous correspondence.

For legal reasons all Inventors receive a standard response, should you wish to clarify this further please contact us using the above freephone number.

May I thank you for contacting us and if I can be of any help in the future please do not hesitate to contact me.

Yours Sincerely

Donna Laister
Hasbro Consumer Affairs

0275316C
Mr Perrson
54 The Bourne
HASTINGS
East Sussex
TN34 3AY

Nicola Joy & Karina Evans

24 January 06

Steven Spielberg
DreamWorks S K G
Universal city
CA91608
U.S.A

Dear Mr Spielberg

Your films are brilliant and so are we. This month we have decided that we want to be film stars, and as you are a well-known director we thought we would approach you first. We are giving you the unique opportunity to employ us to star in your next film. In a nutshell, we are young, gorgeous and photogenic we can pull more than one facial expression (we are yet to have botox) and can even put on a couple of strange voices. We are sure you will agree the above description shows us to be very talented, if you think that's good just wait until you actually meet us. We would like to be invited to your next casting session so we can show you our amazing acting skills and strange voices. We work for a reasonable fee; about eight million pounds apiece would be more than plentiful. We are also a pleasure to work with, as we don't make too many diva like demands. We only ask that a foot masseuse, white balloons, finger buffet of celery sticks and fat free dips are provided wherever we happen to grace the set.

We will now eagerly await your reply. We would appreciate it greatly if you would inform us immediately if you do not wish to exploit this unique opportunity that we have laid before you. If you do not want to use us we are going to approach Mr Jackson.

Yours with anticipation

Nicola Joy A.K.A The naked fork*

Karina Evans A.K.A the partially clothed table mat*

* The above names are remnants from the days we spent in the rock band Café Salacious; we thought we'd keep them as they make exciting screen names.

Gaye Salamander
Roberto Hangadolofosti
Cheap Thrills R Us

New Product Manager
Debenhams
1 Welbeck Street
London
W1G OAA

Dear Sir/Madam

We are writing in hope of interesting you in our latest fashion concept. We are budding fashion designers and have previously sold some of our items in the Netherlands. Our range is aimed at the more depraved amongst society. We would like to offer you some shirts with a twist. Our shirts have been specially adapted to deliver a harsh yet pleasant electrical shock; courtesy of discreet electrified nipple clamps. With these clamps the wearer can receive cheap trills throughout the day, likewise if they have been naughty they can administer them as self-punishment, courtesy of a button disguised as a cuff link. We are sure that this design will be very popular and we are hoping that you will be broadminded enough to consider stocking our shirt, and help us to bring pleasurable pain to the masses.

The electrical device is perfectly safe; a leading electronics company designed it. The device is also detachable, as it is necessary to remove it before washing the garment.

We would greatly appreciate it if you would let us know the outcome of your decision as soon as possible; we are offering you these shirts exclusively and will not offer them to any other company until we have received your correspondence.

Thank you for your time. We look forward to hearing from you soon.

Yours faithfully

Gaye Salamander

Roberto Hangadolofosti

DEBENHAMS

1 Welbeck Street
London
W1G 0AA
T:
www.debenhams.com

Gaye Salamander
Roberto Hangandolofosti
Cheap thrills R' us

24 May 2006

Dear Mr Hangadolofosti

I acknowledge receipt of your letter and would like to thank you for introducing your
company.

Debenhams are currently reviewing the information you kindly sent us and should we be
interested in your proposal, we will contact you shortly with a decision.

Once again, thank you for taking the time to contact us.

Yours sincerely,

Claire Attewell
Customer Relations Department

Debenhams Recall plc. Registered in England. Company no.83395. Registered office 1 Welbeck Street, London W1G 0AA.

Section
4

Marbles? What marbles?

KARINA EVANS
NICOLA JOY
OF JOY-EVANS FAME

Mr Bruce Willis
Ex-husband of Demi Moore
Hollywood
U S of A

15 May 2005

Dear 'The' Willis,

We love your peaches. We are disturbed. It is your fault. We used to be two svelte, beautiful 11 year olds. That is until you came bounding onto our screens with your cheeky eyes and naughty bottom. Since we learnt how to, the mere sight of you has had us covering inanimate objects with chocolate and licking it off whilst fantasising that aforementioned inanimate object is your beautiful appendage.

This enjoyable yet calorific extra-curricular activity has rendered us fat. With sticky table legs.

Today is a turning point. We have realised that beach weather is a-looming, yet our bodies are pasty and wobbly. We have been dieting and exercising frantically for the 7 and a half minutes prior to penning this letter, and would like to courteously invite you to the grand unveiling of our new, aesthetically pleasing beach bodies. We are now beautiful 45 year olds, and true beauty needs to be shared. The great unveiling will take place at outside Hastings Town Hall on 15 July 2005. We look forward to seeing you there. Please find enclosed a photograph of your beautiful self for you to sign if you would be so kind.

Yours with peachy bottoms and deluded minds,

[signature]

KARINA EVANS

[signature]

NICOLI JOY

Whoops, we accidentally sent him a picture of Sylvester Stallone.

SHARON FRUTE
JOANNA KING

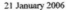

21 January 2006

Mr R Williams
C/O EMI Records
43 Brook Green
London
W6 7EF

Dear Sir/Madam,

We are writing to you regarding an artist that you work with, by the name of Mr
Robbie Williams.

We are interested in Mr Williams as an artist, and although his last album was
undoubtedly his best ever, we feel that he needs some help before he can reach the
pinnacle of his career. We are writing to you so that you can pass an offer of
hospitality onto Mr Williams on our behalf. He is more than welcome to stay with us
for a while, whilst he finds himself. We are not believers in finding the answer to life
at the bottom of a bottle or packet of cigarettes. We will endeavour to rid Mr Williams
of any evils that he may be indulging in, and give him our expert advice in a
comfortable homely rehabilitation environment.

This intensive treatment involves various teas, Earl Grey being a particular favourite
of ours, woolly clothing, and a variety of distraction techniques in the form of non-
violent, non-sexual, clergy themed films.

We have one space available at the moment. We are certain that this is the right
environment for Mr Williams to find and heal himself.

Please contact us as soon as possible regarding this opportunity, as if Mr Williams is
not interested than we have a number of other people to approach.

Yours sincerely,

S FRUTE

J L KING

Henrietta & Gordon Bearbottom

06/03/2006

Morrison Supermarkets PLC
Parry Lane
Bradford
BD4 8TD

Dear Customer Support Department

We find shopping stressful, supermarkets are to blame; this is why:

- We don't like strip lighting; it hurts our eyes as well as making us look crap, parched and ugly.

- Aisles are too narrow and forever clogged up with gossiping old people and boisterous children.

- Trolley wheels drive us insane, they never all move in the same direction at any one time.

- The amount of toxic additives found in food upon the shelves is enough to create a thirty-five foot long tumour.

- The queues are too long at the check out and the bleeping of the scanners is enough to drive anyone insane.

- Our midget regularly gets trampled.

What are you going to do about this? Please reply to the above address.

Henrietta & Gordon Bearbottom

JESS WILLIS-WILLIEMS
NATASHA ASHER

30 January 2006

BCS English Proofreading Service
9 Hames Lane
Newton Regis
Tamworth
B79 0NH

Dear sir/madam;

We are very interested in careers as proof readers as we have just finished taking our english GCSE's and enjoyed them immensely, we are not sure how to go about this and was hoping that you could assist us with this. We have researched several company's on the internet and feel that your the right one for us, we have alot of experience with writing as our GCSE's involved alot of coursework which had to be read several times before submission. We would really appreciate it if you could send us information on how to apply for jobs with yourselves, if not then any information on how to get started in this business will be helpful.

Thank you very much for your time & help.,

Yours Sincerely,

J WILLIS-WILLIEMS
N ASHER

dear

C°l in

We Are GIMP

WE aRe DevianT

wE ArE dEGenEraTe

WE aRe TAKING over The

W⊕RLD

D° you LiKE OuR

PANT?

Sectioned

229

Help

In case you were wondering...

Nicola and Karina simultaneously married Colin Farrell, up a tree in a non-legally binding ceremony. Without his knowledge or consent.

The New York Fire Department neglected to turn up. It got very hot in those padded cat costumes.

The gimp has since returned from Brazil, after extensive cosmetic surgery. He is still rather angry and now gets his jollies dancing around campfires with colonies of mythological creatures.

The midget has still not fully recovered the strength in his tiny jaw, although he has been observed biting his next-door neighbour's poodle. He is hoping to find employment picking forest mushrooms for a well-known company with the elves and pixies.

Due to perm appointments no one turned up for the grand unveiling, sorry Bruce.

And if you're really lucky and gaze skywards on a starry night, you may capture a brief glimpse of Captain Fun leaping across the rooftops of suburbia.

...We Are Disturbed. We will return.

For all of you who didn't reply. What are you? Hmmm? We think that you're all bastards.

More fool you ar*eho*es, we'll switch brands, change companies and visit different establishments.

We feel it our duty to fool the general public.

Stranger than fiction: The little book of alcohol *by Nicola & Karina of Joy-Evans Fame*

In the 1950s one shot of strong Russian vodka would be enough to put you on the fast track to a cirrhotic liver and kill off at least 500,000 brain cells. Due to evolution, brains and liver now have small bunion-like growths, thus ensuring adequate protection against strong Russian vodka.

An Argentinean got his appendage stuck under a man hole cover after the voices in his head told him there was vodka down there and he would be able to slurp it up in the manner of an anteater.

If you leave a certain brand of cider in a large green goblet and place in a cupboard under a strong lamp (in the manner of growing hash), within 6 weeks and 1 day it will be covered in purple mushrooms.

Beer soaked bread will make the pigeons sing louder.

Heated to 35 degrees vermouth starts to solidify and if smeared over the top of a tent makes excellent tarpaulin.

We sincerely hope you didn't believe any of that coz it was all a bunch of crap. (To be hidden at end of book)

If you have enjoyed this book and have any comments
or suggestions to make, please email
disturbed@crombiejardine.com

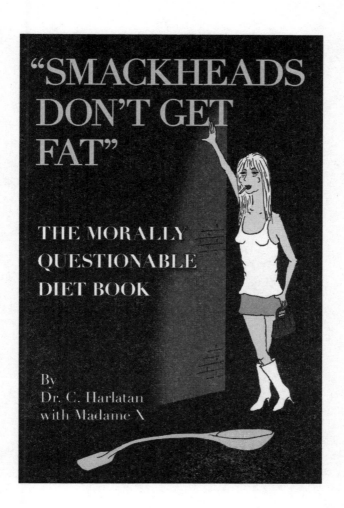

"SMACKHEADS DON'T GET FAT"

THE MORALLY QUESTIONABLE DIET BOOK

By
Dr. C. Harlatan
with Madame X

1-905102-70-4
£7.99

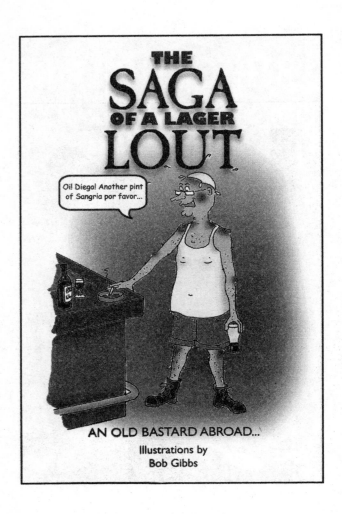

AN OLD BASTARD ABROAD...

Illustrations by
Bob Gibbs

1-905102-82-8
£4.99

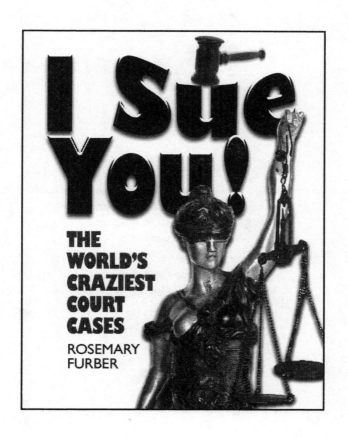

I Sue You!

THE
WORLD'S
CRAZIEST
COURT
CASES

ROSEMARY
FURBER

1-905102-92-5
£4.99

www.crombiejardine.com